FROM

PLAN TO REALITY

THREE

FROM
PLAN TO REALITY
THREE

A THIRD REPORT OF PROGRESS, 1929–1941

ON THE DEVELOPMENT OF THE

NEW YORK–NEW JERSEY–CONNECTICUT METROPOLITAN REGION

INCLUDING DETAILS FOR THE PERIOD STARTING 1937

AND A PROGRAM OF PROPOSALS FOR

POST-WAR PUBLIC WORKS

REGIONAL PLAN ASSOCIATION, INC.

400 MADISON AVENUE, NEW YORK CITY

REGIONAL PLAN ASSOCIATION

OFFICERS

GEORGE MCANENY
Chairman of the Board

FREDERICK C. HORNER
President

LAWSON PURDY
Vice-President

BERTRAM SAUNDERS
Vice-President

KENNETH A. IVES
Treasurer

C. MCKIM NORTON
Executive Vice-President

FREDERICK P. CLARK*
Planning Director

FRANCES PERRY
Secretary

HAROLD M. LEWIS, *Consultant***

DIRECTORS

TECHNICAL STAFF

C. EARL MORROW, *Planning Engineer*

GEORGE A. SCHILLER, *Assistant Engineer*

Charles L. Austin†

George A. Hay, Jr.

PAUL A. FROELICH, *Assistant Engineer*

Charles Herrick

Walter A. Wachter

PUBLIC RELATIONS

O'BRIEN BOLDT, *Editor*

* Joined the staff April 1, 1942.
** Was Chief Engineer and Secretary to November 1, 1939; Chief Engineer and Planning Officer to April 1, 1941; since that date Consultant to the Association.
† Entered military service, U. S. Army, March, 1941.

FOREWORD

THIS IS THE THIRD in a series of reports on the development of the physical aspects of the New York-New Jersey-Connecticut metropolitan region and, incidentally, the evolution of local, county, state, and Federal planning as a means of guiding such development.

The first and second volumes of FROM PLAN TO REALITY together cover the eight-year period immediately following the publication, in 1929, of the REGIONAL PLAN OF NEW YORK AND ITS ENVIRONS. The present report brings the story down another five years and through 1941, reprinting in book form four Regional Plan Bulletins supplemented by additional material not heretofore published.

In a metropolis composed of parts of three states, 22 counties and 495 autonomous municipal units, coordinated action in matters of regional importance cannot be achieved without tremendous effort. The Regional Plan has played its part in the developments summarized in this report by presenting throughout a broad pattern of regional development, a mosaic incorporating many plans originating from many sources. The Regional Plan Association has also served in keeping the Plan up-to-date and workable, and in stimulating planning as a natural forerunner of action on matters of regional importance. Most of the credit for concrete accomplishments is due, however, to those able and energetic public officials who, from time to time, overcame the inertia of established routine to acquire new parks and playgrounds, to forge new links in the chain of regional highways and parkways, to construct new housing units, and to build new airports, markets and other terminals.

The great metropolis which surrounds the Port of New York has passed, in five years, from a period of depression to the hectic activity of a second World War. Construction of new public facilities has virtually ceased. Until the war is won, our problem is to use what we have to the limit of capacity. Certainly the regional plans brought to reality since the inception of the studies of the Committee on the Regional Plan twenty-one years ago, have made the Region immeasurably more effective for the manufacture and movement of the supplies of war.

Looking to the future, there remain great developments to be accomplished throughout the Region. A post-war construction program to meet some of the most urgent regional needs of parks, parkways and highways, is set forth in the appropriate chapters of this volume. Speaking in general terms, more progress has been achieved through our previous effort in transportation and public services than in the less spectacular phases of neighborhood development within the appropriate settings of regional highways, railways, water supply, and sanitation facilities. The rebuilding of the Region's central cities into communities suitable for well-rounded family life at all ranges of income has indeed become the greatest challenge lying ahead.

GEORGE MCANENY

August, 1942

TABLE OF CONTENTS

C O N T E N T S

MAPS AND DIAGRAMS

PHOTOGRAPHIC ILLUSTRATIONS

PHOTOGRAPHIC ILLUSTRATIONS

LIST OF TABLES

I. INTRODUCTION

The second World War has emphasized in many ways the importance of viewing the metropolitan area centering around the Port of New York as a single unit. Available maps, studies and proposals of the Region as a whole, through the various reports and unpublished data of the Regional Plan Association and its predecessor, have proved helpful in developing emergency programs.

A report of the regional development of this area is important at this time not so much in itself as for laying a groundwork upon which to build for the future and in adjusting the proposals for highways, parks and other major physical features as published in the Graphic Regional Plan in the light of the present-day outlook for future needs.

With the publication of the 1940 population Census, it has become evident that under peace-time conditions the Region is tending to approach a stable population. The era of mushroom growth of cities, with the doubling of their populations within short periods of time, is over but there will continue to be shifts within the Region resulting in growth or decay in certain areas. The extent to which the war will stimulate the development of permanent new war industries in other parts of the Nation and thus further retard the industrial growth of the New York Region is still problematical.

Recognition of these new trends offers both a challenge and an opportunity to planning agencies. It gives them hope that they can develop plans which will offer permanent solutions to problems of transportation and congestion, which previously had seemed to grow faster than a solution could be provided. On the other hand, it presents an urgent problem of conservation of resources through curtailing the growth of blight and loss of values in the older built-up areas and of finding practical plans for the rebuilding and conversion of these areas as an asset rather than a liability to the community.

This report constitutes a revised Graphic Plan so far as regional proposals for major highways, parkways and parks are concerned and lays the basis for the post-war public works program by showing the most urgent gaps in the present systems of such facilities. In general, it may be said that the original pattern for the physical development of the Region, as published in 1929, continues to be carried out in many of its elements ahead of schedule, on the basis of the forty-year program that was then contemplated.

SUMMARY OF PROGRESS

This introductory Chapter is devoted to a brief summary of the progress reported in the succeeding chapters. Programs for post-war development are summarized at the end of the chapters on highways and on parks and parkways.

General Traffic Highways (Chapter III)

For the purpose of this report progress on highways is defined to include those projects which have received official preliminary action in the way of studies or adoption of projects, in addition to those completed or under construction. A mileage summary of progress on the various classifications of routes in the regional system is given on the back of the map facing page III-4. Statistics are given through 1940, with emphasis on developments during the preceding four years.

Outstanding event of the period under review has been the extent of development on Inner Routes of the regional system. On a percentage basis of mileage involved in this classification, construction of these has exceeded all other types of routes. The degree of relief afforded the central portion of the Region, where traffic has always increased faster than facilities could be provided, is incalculable.

The vital river crossings in the network of Inner Routes completed since 1929 in accordance with the regional system include two new Hudson River crossings and the Triborough and Whitestone bridges and Queens Midtown Tunnel across the East River. Serving these new facilities, many miles of new approach roads have been constructed, forming the essential inner elements for a coordinated system of highways.

Radiating from the Inner Routes many new arterials have been completed or, in some instances, plans for their development adopted, thus assuring their ultimate realization. Despite radical improvement in regional motor travel, potential benefits of development to date cannot be fully realized until other proposals of the highway system are put into effect.

Of particular significance to regional motor travel is advancement of the Metropolitan Highway Loop, principal element in the regional system of major routes. At present, excluding sections over existing roads and a parallel parkway, over 41 per cent of its total length has been constructed, 6 per cent having taken place during the four years ending with 1940. More important than any linear measurement of the Loop's development is the fact that the underlying theory of its function has been accepted by officials responsible for highway construction and also by the motoring public.

Standards of road construction have continued to improve as a general extension of refinements previously adopted. These include wider lanes, flatter curves, longer sight distances, separation of opposing traffic lanes and grade separations at intersections with other major routes.

New York State has made preliminary studies for limited access highways under enabling legislation adopted in 1937, and the New Jersey State Chamber of Commerce has sponsored similar legislation for New Jersey.

Parks and Parkways (Chapter II)

Acquisition and development of recreational lands have taken place at an encouraging pace in the sector of the Region east of the Hudson River. In New Jersey, progress has been slow when compared with developments in Long Island and Westchester County. Several agencies in New Jersey, however, have been active in laying the groundwork for a comprehensive recreational system in that state. In other parts of the Region principal advances during the past five years have been the continued physical improvement or reconstruction of park lands with the use of Work Projects Administration personnel.

Most impressive park advances in the way of development and expansion have occurred in New York City. Considerable acreage has been added to the city's parks by the reclamation of marshy and under-water land. The development schedule has provided active recreation for all age groups.

The wide use of Westchester and Long Island parkways created a serious problem at the city boundaries. During the past five years these have been extended in and through the city. Worthy of special note is construction of the Belt Parkway, which skirts the intensively developed portions of Brooklyn and Queens and parallels the Metropolitan Loop for its entire length on Long Island.

Rail and Port Development (Chapter IV, pages 1 to 5)

The outstanding physical improvement to the trunk line railroad system has been the completion of the West Side freight line in Manhattan. The Port of New York Authority has, however, advanced its studies of two important elements of the proposed regional railroad system—a freight tunnel under Upper New York Bay and a suburban rapid transit system to serve Northern New Jersey.

The elimination of 68 railroad grade crossings throughout the Region during the period under review has greatly facilitated the safe movement of highway traffic. In New York City, construction of a program to make the city completely free of railroad grade intersections was undertaken and was scheduled for completion by 1943; construction of several projects has been withheld due to war demands for materials. Unification of New York City's rapid transit lines has enabled officials to clear the streets of many miles of ancient elevated structures in Brooklyn and Manhattan.

The problem of terminal facilities for buses and trucks serving the Port of New York has been recognized and plans advanced for their development. Plans for a publicly owned produce terminal to expedite transfer and distribution of produce have been studied by officials to replace Washington Market. A wholesale poultry market on Newtown Creek in Queens has been completed by the City of New York and a farmers' produce market is under construction in the Canarsie section of Brooklyn.

Improvement of New York harbor and navigable waterways in various parts of the Region has been continued. Other port development has centered around providing facilities for Army and Navy use.

Air Transportation (Chapter IV, pages 5 to 8)

Most spectacular among recent transportation developments in the Region was the great increase in commercial flying across both the Atlantic and overland routes. Principal progress during the past four years in providing major terminal facilities for commercial flying has been completion of LaGuardia Field, the resumption of service from Newark Airport and the start of construction of Idlewild Airport in Queens to replace Floyd Bennett Field recently taken over by the Navy. Under pressure of defense requirements many other airports of the regional system have been or are being developed on a scale which dwarfs former accomplishment. Every indication points to the full utilization of these facilities in the post-war years. It is also clear that aviation will create future problems of a new character through post-war inheritance of aircraft production plants, and flying and ground personnel.

Water Supply and Sanitation (Chap. IV, pp. 8 to 12)

Substantial progress has been made on the development of a new source of water supply for New York City from the tributaries of the Hudson and Delaware rivers.

Appointment of a new commission to study ways and means to meet the water shortage in metropolitan

New Jersey has been the principal accomplishment on the part of New Jersey officials. More recently a plan, interconnecting existing water systems, has been worked out as a measure to meet any war-time emergency.

Considerable effort has been expended by the Interstate Sanitation Commission to bring about an understanding by a large number of communities of the necessity as well as the desirability of constructing sewage treatment works in the interest of abatement of harbor pollution. During 1941 the commission's control was extended to include the Connecticut shore when that state signed the interstate pact.

Construction of a comprehensive program of sewage treatment in New York City is well under way. The effect of plants placed in operation within recent years has improved boundary waters and in some instances afforded necessary protection to enable development of new waterfront parks such as Sound View Park in The Bronx.

Outside of New York City, development of municipal and jointly operated treatment plants has taken place, particularly in the Hackensack River valley. Several notable improvements and extensions have been completed in carrying out the comprehensive sewerage plan of Westchester County.

Public Housing (Chapter IV, pages 11 and 12)

A major factor in stimulating construction of low rent public housing during the past five years was the United States Housing Authority. Operating under a three-year authorization to subsidize local projects, a request for additional funds was turned down by Congress in 1939.

Federal money was not solely responsible for all public housing in the Region. New York City provided its Housing Authority with funds obtained by special taxes to be used to service Authority bonds. On a broader scale, New York State was enabled by legislative act, effective January 1, 1939, to obtain funds through the sale of bonds, to be loaned to municipalities for low rent housing on a 60-year amortization basis. In New Jersey about 10 per cent of the funds for projects were raised by local housing authorities set up with the cooperation of the State Housing Authority. Public housing projects completed in the Region in 1941 included 28 in New Jersey, 18 in New York City, four in New York State outside of New York City, and ten in Connecticut.

Zoning (Chapter V)

As a means of regulating private development, zoning spread rapidly and continuously in the 1930-1940 decade. By the end of that period 351 of the 495 municipalities of the Region had adopted zoning ordinances. This represented 55 per cent of the total area of the Region with 96 per cent of its total population living under zoning protection. Zoning regulations had been adopted in at least six additional municipalities in the Region by the end of 1941.

While the rapid application of zoning to areas formerly unregulated is an indication of progress, much of it cannot be regarded as fulfilling desired objectives. However, recent trends throughout the Region show an increasing tendency to correct faulty zoning by incorporating modern standards, either by the adoption of new ordinances or by the comprehensive revision of old ordinances. Increase in control of population density, outdoor advertising and the more intensive uses of land, and provision for offstreet parking and loading of motor vehicles are some of the more progressive zoning practices.

Planning Agencies (Chapter VI)

New planning agencies, notably the New York City Planning Commission, commenced to function in the five-year period under review, and some planning agencies moved toward the goal of wise community development through coordination of developmental activities of the governing unit and private enterprise. At the same time it was becoming increasingly clear that many local planning boards were relatively inactive, that the formula of a spare-time commission, operating with no staff and small appropriations, is inadequate for a competent planning job, and that many boards' conception of their function is too narrowly limited.

A shift in the center of gravity of planning activity was apparent as Federal agencies, together with their regional and local branches, increased in number and scope and revealed a strong tendency to incorporate the planning approach in their operations. State planning agencies also gained strength, with increased emphasis on basic economic problems and closer collaboration with other state agencies. County planning boards, although failing of establishment in several counties following WPA planning study projects, gave convincing demonstration of their worth in a few counties where a full-time staff was set up.

JOHNSON PARK, MIDDLESEX COUNTY—FIRST STEP TOWARD A RARITAN RIVER PARKWAY

II. PARKS AND PARKWAYS

The nineteenth century concept of a park as a sylvan retreat in the midst of a city or a controlled wilderness at the city's edge has yielded to the demand, in more recent years, that park systems provide recreation within physical and financial reach of the city's population and protection for residential areas. Parks are no longer a municipal luxury, but have become recognized as a vital urban facility, as essential to the health and stability of the community as schools, hospitals or utilities.

The Regional Plan, with full recognition of the factors involved, proposed in 1929 a three-fold system of parks for the New York Metropolitan Region devised to provide complete public recreational facilities. It included public beaches and large reservations in the environs connected by parkways and boulevards to population centers for all-day or week-end excursions; a number of city parks large enough to include active and passive recreation within walking distance or rapid transit ride from densely settled areas; and, perhaps most important of all, the development of a complete local park and playground system located with reference to population and residential areas.

The purpose of this Bulletin is to record the progress made in the Region's public recreation system since 1928 with emphasis on the years 1937 to 1940 inclusive,[1] and in the light of this background and current conditions of world war to offer a program for the immediate future and the post-war period.

The two years of "prosperity" and ten years of "depression" included in the period under review have witnessed unprecedented park and parkway development in the Region together with a surprising increase in numbers of people who participate in outdoor recreation throughout the Nation. Expressed in terms of area, there has been a gain of more than 40 per cent over the Region's 94,000 park acres in 1928. The sum of $241,999,692 was spent in New York City alone for capital park expenditures in the three years 1934, 1935 and 1936.[1] As indices of increased use of recreation facilities total revenue from facilities in New York City parks, including fees and concessions, doubled during the twelve-year period, reaching a total of over a million dollars in 1940.

Turning from the recent past to the immediate future a different picture presents itself. The world is in the midst of a war period. In 1935, 60 per cent of average expenditures for park operation and maintenance in 1,071 cities of the United States came from emergency or relief funds.[2] Such funds, together with city park maintenance budgets, will of necessity be reduced as the national defense program advances. Defense priorities of capital, labor and materials will reduce the possibility of park and playground development. Adequate maintenance of existing facilities is threatened.

To recognize the factors involved in the immediate future, however, does not preclude looking forward to the post-war period when the transition from a war to a peace economy will call for an expansion of public works including park projects. Plans should be made, lands acquired, programs evolved now in preparation for peace. A program for acquisition and

[1] See FROM PLAN TO REALITY (1933) and FROM PLAN TO REALITY, Two (1938) published by Regional Plan Association, Inc., for detailed analysis of the periods 1928-1932 and 1933-1936 respectively.

[1] MUNICIPAL AND COUNTY PARKS IN THE UNITED STATES (1935), U. S. Department of the Interior in cooperation with National Recreation Association, page 132.
[2] *Ibid.,* page 40.

FROM PLAN TO REALITY—THREE

TABLE I.—PARK STATISTICS, BY COUNTIES WITHIN NEW YORK AND ITS ENVIRONS, SHOWING ACQUISITIONS, 1936 TO 1940[1]

County	Area in acres, 1936	Acquisitions 1936-1940, acres	Area in 1940		Per cent of increase, 1936-1940	Total proposed system, acres
			Acres	Per cent of county		
NEW YORK STATE						
Bronx	4,400	1,080	5,480	20.7	24.5	6,082
Kings (Brooklyn)	3,470	1,769	5,239	11.9	51.0	5,892
New York (Manhattan)	2,345	71	2,416	17.2	3.0	2,416
Queens	4,519	1,359	5,878	8.5	30.1	9,622
Richmond	2,704	337	3,041	8.3	12.5	4,526
Total New York City	17,438	4,616	22,054	11.6	26.5	28,538
Dutchess (Part of)	406	0	406	.5	0	6,081
Nassau	11,580	69	11,649	6.7	.6	22,140
Orange (Part of)	22,084	0	22,084	8.3	0	39,768
Putnam	3,646	0	3,646	2.4	0	11,840
Rockland	18,503	1,231	19,734	16.8	6.7	37,849
Suffolk	15,986	1,009	16,995	2.9	6.3	53,722
Westchester	17,975	15	17,990	6.3	.1	24,668
Total New York State	107,618	6,940	114,558	6.2	6.4	224,705
NEW JERSEY						
Bergen	2,318	0	2,318	1.5	0	31,808
Essex	4,177	352	4,529	5.6	8.4	6,404
Hudson	758	41	799	2.9	5.4	1,943
Middlesex	345	1,024	1,369	.7	296.8	7,749
Monmouth (Part of)	17	709	726	.3	4,170.6	11,976
Morris	1,406	0	1,406	.5	0	13,937
Passaic	1,456	112	1,568	1.3	7.7	19,653
Somerset	112	0	112	.1	0	11,072
Union	4,389	139	4,528	6.9	3.2	8,123
Total New Jersey	14,978	2,377	17,355	1.2	16.0	112,665
CONNECTICUT						
Fairfield (Part of)	2,290	79	2,369	.9	3.4	20,315
Total for Region	124,886	9,396	134,282	3.8	7.5	357,685

[1] Excluding all parks of less than one acre in area.

TABLE II.—PARK STATISTICS FOR SEVEN METROPOLITAN REGIONS, 1930 COMPARED WITH 1940

Region	Park acreage		Per cent increase	Population		Population per acre of park		Area of Region, square miles	Per cent of Region in parks, 1940
	1930	1940		1930	1940	1930	1940		
New York	108,660	134,282	23.6	11,458,004	12,308,350	105.4	91.7	5,528	3.8
Chicago	52,500	63,450	20.8	5,058,147	5,235,369	96.3	82.5	7,817	1.3
Detroit	5,554	6,578	18.4	2,262,147	2,479,002	407.2	376.8	3,250	0.3
Boston[1]	14,118	16,724	18.5	1,905,408	1,924,710	135.0	115.0	398	6.6
Cleveland[2]	10,000	12,200	22.0	1,201,455	1,217,250	120.1	99.8	453	4.2
Buffalo[3]	3,609	4,993	38.3	762,408	798,377	211.3	159.9	1,034	0.8
Cincinnati[4]	3,200	5,307	65.8	589,356	620,000	184.2	116.8	405	2.1

[1] Includes all under supervision of the Metropolitan District Commission in 1940 and those under the jurisdiction of the Park Department of the City of Boston in 1939.
[2] 2,300 additional park acres outside of the Region but in the Metropolitan Park System. Figures given only for Cuyahoga County.
[3] Figures are for the part of the Region in Erie County.
[4] That part of the Region in Hamilton County.

TABLE III.—PARK STATISTICS FOR CITIES OF MORE THAN 500,000 POPULATION, 1930 COMPARED WITH 1940

City	Park acreage		Per cent increase	Population		Population per acre of park		Area of city, square miles	Per cent of area in parks[5]
	1930	1940		1930	1940	1930	1940		
New York	14,079	22,054	56.6	6,930,446	7,380,259	492	335	299.0	11.6
Chicago	5,958	6,668	11.9	3,376,438	3,384,556	567	508	206.7	5.0
Philadelphia	7,859	7,957	1.2	1,950,961	1,935,086	248	243	127.2	9.8
Detroit	3,193	3,950	23.7	1,568,662	1,618,549	491	410	139.0	4.5
Los Angeles	5,412	6,098[1]	12.7	1,238,048	1,496,792	229	245	448.3	2.1
Cleveland	3,160	3,887	23.0	900,429	878,385	285	226	73.1	8.3
Baltimore	3,475	3,648[1]	5.0	804,874	854,144	232	234	78.7	7.2
St. Louis	2,956	3,248[1]	9.8	821,960	813,748	278	251	61.0	8.3
Boston	2,918	3,780[1]	29.5	781,188	769,520	268	204	43.9	13.5
Pittsburgh	1,869	1,987	6.3	669,817	665,384	358	335	52.1	6.1
Washington	4,000[2]	7,391[1]	84.8	486,869	663,153	122	90	61.4	18.8
San Francisco	2,897	4,621	59.5	634,394	629,553	219	136	44.6	16.2
Milwaukee	1,292	1,746[3]	35.1	578,249	589,558	448	331	43.4	6.3
Buffalo	1,598[4]	2,321[1]	45.2	573,076	575,150	359	248	39.4	9.2

[1] 1939 area. [2] Approximate. [3] 1935 area. [4] 1926 area. [5] Based on latest figures available as given in column 2.

Courtesy, Connecticut State Highway Department

THE MERRITT PARKWAY IN THE TOWN OF GREENWICH

development of parks and parkways of regional importance is included herein; similar programs for local and neighborhood facilities should be developed by the various municipalities.

PARK ACQUISITION AND DEVELOPMENT

Measured by the acreage acquired, park progress in the past four years has not kept pace with the rate of expansion in the eight years immediately preceding. Between 1936 and 1940 a total of 9,396 acres has been added to the park system, which amounts to about 23.5 per cent of the 40,003 acres added in the whole twelve-year period. Economic conditions can be cited as partly responsible for this but a failure to realize the importance of a substantial park and parkway program in some of the deficient areas may be said to constitute another major reason.

While development of park lands is often essential to obtain the full recreational value of a site, acquisition of the land may be said to be the major concern of regional planning and is therefore measured in greater detail than development. Where parkways are involved, their construction also belongs in a regional program. Much of the land acquired in a previous period has been developed in the past four years. Bear Mountain Park and many of the parks in New York City such as Pelham Bay, Jacob Riis and the Marine parks in Brooklyn and Staten Island, afford examples of recent development in older areas.

Progress on 1937 Program

A list of projects on which some type of action was urgently needed was presented in 1937.[1] There were

[1] Information Bulletin No. 39, "Important Projects in the Region Needing Immediate Attention," December 6, 1937, page 3.

eight new park areas suggested for acquisition at an early date and six parkways suggested for adoption and mapping or acquisition.

Of the eight park areas, progress in land acquisition was made on three, additional studies were made on two and no action was taken on the remaining three. Following is a list of the projects and the action taken:

Park Areas	Action
Along the Top of the Palisades	Additional parcels acquired
North Shore of Jamaica Bay	Adopted in City Master Plan and acquired
Along Merritt Parkway	No additional lands along parkway
Oceanfront Parks in Monmouth County	Additional studies and promotional work
Newark Bay Waterfront	No action
Watchung Mountains	No action
Overpeck Creek Meadows	Adopted on Master Plan of Bergen County
Long Island Motor Parkway in Queens	Acquired and developed as bicycle trail

Construction progress on parkways is described later on in this report.

General Progress in the Region

On the whole, park progress in the past four years in the Region has not been disappointing in view of economic conditions. The advance is not uniformly distributed over the whole area, some districts being highly active and others practically at a standstill.

In Figure 1 the upper diagram shows how the Region as a whole is falling behind in a schedule that would complete the regional system by 1965. New York City, on the other hand, is ahead of schedule. In the lower diagram of the same illustration it may be seen that park expansion has more than kept up with population increase in the Region and particularly so in the City of New York.

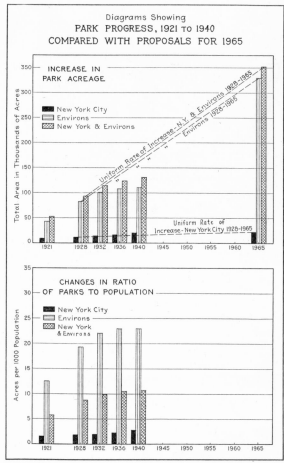

Diagrams Showing
PARK PROGRESS, 1921 TO 1940
COMPARED WITH PROPOSALS FOR 1965

FIGURE 1

In Table I (page 2) the amounts added to the various county acreages in the past four years are tabulated and related to existing and proposed quantities. For the Region as a whole nearly 9,400 acres have been added which is an increase of about 7.5 per cent. Fairfield County added only 79 acres, or 3.4 per cent, to its 1936 acreage. New Jersey added 2,377 acres, or 16 per cent. New York State increased its acreage by 6,940 of which 4,616 acres are in New York City. By far the most impressive park progress in the Region in the past four years, both in the way of expansion and development, has occurred in New York City under the leadership of Park Commissioner Robert Moses.

Comparison with Other Regions and Cities

It is of interest to compare recent progress in park acquisition in the New York Region with that of other regions and cities of the Nation. For this Tables II and III (page 2) were prepared. The difference in size and population of the areas involved makes it necessary to compare ratios of park land to population.

Table II lists figures for seven regional areas. It is observed from this table that of those having a population of one million or more, the New York Region heads the list in percentage increase of acreage during the decade ending with 1940. Its acreage of park per person is higher than all regions save Chicago. Many thousands of acres, however, need be added for it to approach the ideal which aims to utilize ten per cent of the Region for parks.

In Table III statistics for cities of more than 500,000 population, fourteen in all, show New York City to be rapidly correcting the grave condition of insufficient recreation area which existed in 1928 at the time the studies of the Committee on a Regional Plan of New York and Its Environs were formally presented to the public. While many completed parks and parkways may be recognized as former Regional Plan pro-

Courtesy, New Jersey Work Projects Administration

DEVELOPMENT IN BOTH NEW AND OLD PARKS ADVANCED BY WPA PROJECTS
Cheesequake State Park (left); Palisades Interstate Park (right).

Courtesy, Department of Parks, City

TYPICAL NEW PLAY FACILITIES IN NEW YORK CITY

Top, marginal playground in Central Park at West 77th Street. Second row: neighborhood playground in Astoria, Queens (left); playground in Sunset Park, Brooklyn (right). Third row, playgrounds along parkways: along Southern Parkway, Queens (left); along the Shore Road section of Belt Parkway, Brooklyn (right). Bottom row, other facilities along parkways: parking and picnic areas at Plum Island (left); overpass and paths for pedestrians and bicycles along Belt Parkway (right).

COUNTY	AREA IN ACRES 1928	ACQUIRED 1928 - 1940	AREA IN 1940 ACRES	PERCENT OF COUNTY % OF COUNTY	PERCENT OF INCREASE	TOTAL PROPOSED SYSTEM
NEW YORK CITY	11747	10307	22054	11.6	87.7	28538
DUTCHESS (PART OF)	6	400	406	.5	6666.6	6081
NASSAU	3890	7759	11649	6.7	199.4	22140
ORANGE (PART OF)	20198	1886	22084	8.3	9.3	39766
PUTNAM	0	3646	3646	2.4	(ALL NEW)	11840
ROCKLAND	17388	2346	19734	16.9	13.5	37948
SUFFOLK	12102	4893	16995	2.9	40.4	53722
WESTCHESTER	17193	797	17990	6.3	4.1	24668
TOTAL STATE OF N Y	82524	31934	114558	6.2	38.7	224705
BERGEN	1158	1160	2318	1.5	100.2	31808
ESSEX	3975	554	4529	5.6	13.9	6404
HUDSON	758	41	799	2.9	5.4	1943
MIDDLESEX	89	1280	1369	.7	1438.2	7749
MONMOUTH (PART OF)	16	710	726	.3	4437.5	11976
MORRIS	107	1299	1406	.5	1214.0	13937
PASSAIC	463	1105	1568	1.3	238.6	19653
SOMERSET	112	0	112	.1	0.0	11072
UNION	4013	515	4528	6.9	12.8	8123
TOTAL STATE OF N J	10691	6664	17355	1.2	62.3	112665
FAIRFIELD (PART OF)	1064	1305	2369	.9	122.5	20315
TOTAL FOR REGION	94279	40003	134282	3.8	42.4	357685

PROGRESS IN PARK ACQUISITION

SOUND

ISLAND

F F O L K

OCEAN

NEW YORK and its ENVIRONS

Showing

D REGIONAL PARK SYSTEM

and

ESS IN ITS ACQUISITION

1928-1940

N ASSOCIATION, INC.   SEPTEMBER 1941   NEW YORK CITY

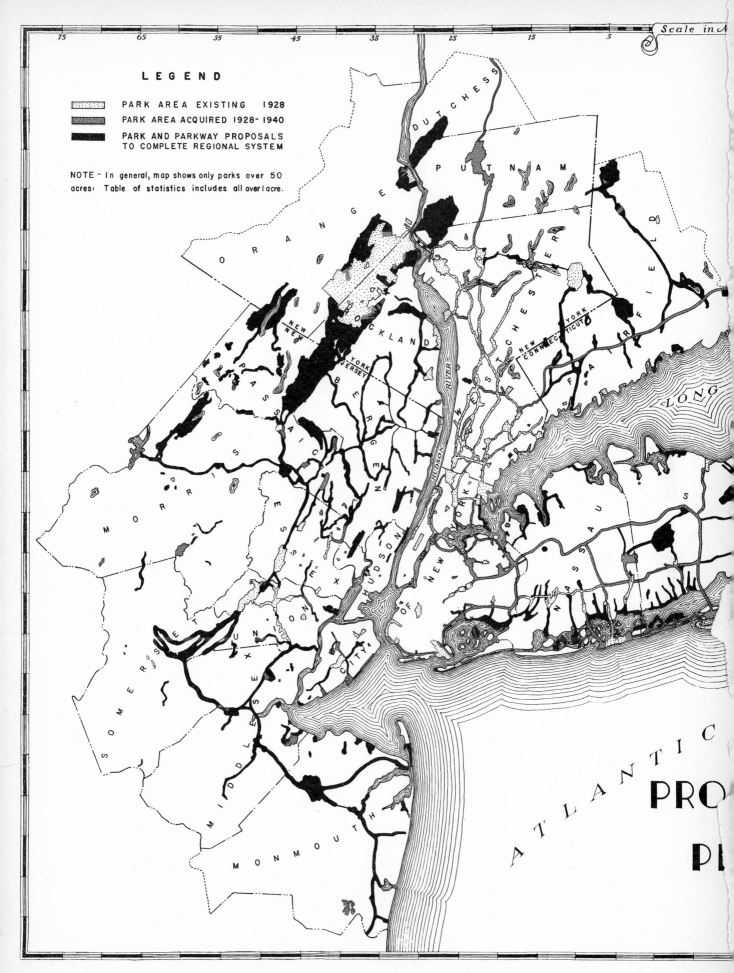

LEGEND

PARK AREA EXISTING 1928
PARK AREA ACQUIRED 1928-1940
PARK AND PARKWAY PROPOSALS
TO COMPLETE REGIONAL SYSTEM

NOTE - In general, map shows only parks over 50
acres: Table of statistics includes all over I acre.

PRO

Pl

FIGURE 2

posals, the credit for their establishment is due the public officials responsible for park development, particularly Robert Moses in his capacity of Chairman of the New York State Council of Parks, President of the Long Island State Park Commission and Commissioner of the Park Department of New York City.

In percentage increase of park area New York City leads all of the fourteen cities listed, with the exception of Washington and San Francisco. Upon examination of the actual acreage acquired, it is found that New York City leads the field with 7,975 new acres which is 4,584 more than its closest competitor, Washington. There is ample room for a further improvement in the ratio of people per park acre. We find there that the only cities with lower acreage standards (that is, more persons per acre of park) than New York are Detroit and Chicago. New York City now has 11.6 per cent of its land area given over to parks.

New Jersey

The part of New Jersey that lies within the Region is notably deficient in the larger type of parks and parkways, as may be seen readily by reference to Figure 2 (facing page 4). There are no completed parkways. Only four counties have park systems. A few scattered state parks, the interstate park along the Palisades, the Morristown National Park and a few large county and municipal parks are all that are of regional importance.

In the past four years the acquisitions include two state parks, one at Cheesequake in Middlesex County and one at Allaire in Monmouth County, and also a few additional parcels of land for the Palisades Parkway in Bergen County and for the existing county system in Union County. The total additions were 2,377 acres compared with 6,664 acres for the 12-year period.

Progress in county parks has continued in the development of already acquired areas by WPA and CCC labor supervised by the county park organizations. Such work consists of clearing, grading and seeding, and construction of roads, paths and various service utilities.

In Essex County, development of park acreage with work relief funds has continued. The following county parks have now been completed: Branch Brook Park Extension, Brookdale Park and Ivy Hill Park.

In Passaic County, development involved WPA projects in bringing the existing parks to completion and putting them in a state of greater usefulness to the public. Notable was the completion of Weasel Brook Park of 23 acres, the general landscape features of Goffle Brook Park of 110 acres, and Dey Mansion, a Washington Headquarters project.

In Union County additional park areas to the extent of 139 acres were acquired during the past four years. With a WPA grant, a construction program of $150,000 was undertaken and completed in 1939, which included restoring several dams and bridges that were destroyed during the excessive rainfall in 1938. In addition to these structures, other improvements were made including field houses, roads, paths and landscaping.

While the acquisition of acreage is not extensive throughout New Jersey there have been several activities preliminary to a broader program which may be recorded as progress. Most of these are state-wide in scope or made by state agencies.

The New Jersey State Planning Board has been active in the further study of parks including the study of an immediate program. A report by the New Jersey Board of Commerce and Navigation which was published in December, 1939, suggested a number of sites along the Atlantic coast for development as waterfront parks. An organization entitled New Jersey Parks and Recreation Association was formed in 1940 to promote parks throughout the state.

Locally the Bergen County Planning Board has been conspicuous in activity looking toward the establishment of a park system. A proposed system has been worked out and was adopted by the Board in 1940 as a part of its master plan. It includes parkways along the Passaic River, Pascack Creek and Hackensack River.

An outstanding example of municipal action is afforded by Fort Lee. As a base for the preparation of a revised zoning ordinance the Board of Liquidation for the Borough of Fort Lee made and adopted a master plan which included a comprehensive program of parks and parkways.

The recreational projects of the New Jersey WPA since July, 1935, in the nine counties in the Region have included the construction, reconstruction or improvement of: 239 recreational buildings; 51 stadiums, grandstands and bleachers; 260 playgrounds; 114 athletic fields; 396 tennis courts; 14 swimming pools; and many other features such as ski jumps, handball courts, wading pools and golf courses.

In New York and Connecticut

Park expansion in New York State outside of New York City but within the Region took place largely in the first eight years of the 12-year period and principally in connection with the establishment of parkways. In the past four years 2,324 acres were acquired compared with 21,627 for the twelve years, most of the recent additions being in Rockland and Suffolk counties. The Eastern State Parkway has been extended beyond the limits of the Region in Dutchess

THE SITE OF FLUSHING MEADOW PARK
Left, the salt marsh before the World's Fair; right, a view of the Fair. See opposite page for subsequent development.

County as has the Merritt Parkway in Fairfield County. The figures quoted do not reflect activity beyond the edge of the Region.

In Rockland County additions to the Palisades Interstate Park constitute the new acreage in the past four years. In Nassau and Suffolk counties progress in that period consisted principally of the development of park and parkway lands acquired previously and is described later. Outstanding additions in these counties are the Bayard-Cutting Arboretum in Islip and a local waterfront park in Oyster Bay.

The 79 acres of new parks reported for the part of Fairfield County, Connecticut, within the Region consist of additions to Wooster Mountain and Sherwood Island state parks.

New York City

In the City of New York the 22,054 acres in parks at present constitute about 11.6 per cent of its total land area. Since 1928 acquisition has amounted to 10,307 acres, the four years preceding 1941 accounting for 44.7 per cent of this.

While the most striking accomplishment of the Park Department has been the development of a system of parkways, noteworthy progress has been made in the expansion of playground and other recreational facilities. Some of these were established on lands along the parkways and were acquired in connection with their development. Projects of the WPA since July, 1935, in

the City of New York have included the construction, reconstruction or improvement of: 40 stadiums, grandstands and bleachers; 352 playgrounds; 59 athletic fields; 422 tennis courts; 18 swimming pools; and many other features such as bandshells, handball courts, wading pools and golf courses. In this period expenditures from WPA and sponsors' funds for recreational facilities constructed by WPA in New York City totalled $197,257,000. Of this amount, $150,065,-000 was expended for wages, and $47,192,000 was spent for non-labor items.

In connection with the construction of the East River Drive considerable tracts of land along the river were reclaimed. The largest of these, the East River Park of about 33 acres, extending from Grand Street to 12th Street between the drive and the river, has been developed for recreational use. A continuation of this park south to Montgomery Street and including the old Corlears Hook Park was being developed in 1940. The addition of this area to the city park system fills a long felt need in this section of the Lower East Side. Other smaller park areas have been created along the drive and the Carl Schurz Park at 86th Street has been extended and improved.

Along the Henry Hudson Parkway a considerable area of shallow water inside the bulkhead lines was filled in and developed as play space. The recreational facilities along the shore west of the parkway roads were made accessible by footways over or under the

Courtesy, Department of Parks, City of New York

FLUSHING MEADOW PARK TODAY

Left, picture of present conditions from same point of view as earlier photographs shown on opposite page; right, close-up of area adjacent to New York City Building.

traffic lanes.

Proposed as a park for many years, the selection of the Flushing Meadows in Queens as the site for the New York World's Fair resulted in its acquisition by the city. With the completion of the Fair, development of the area as one of the large city parks was started immediately. About $50,000,000 worth of basic and permanent improvements remain and will become an integral part of the park.

Important also was the rebuilding and improving of Rockaway Beach and Coney Island. Subject to intense use by the city's teeming millions during the hot summer months, their usefulness was greatly improved by expanding the beaches and providing greater parking space and game areas. While most of the people who use these two beaches travel by the rapid transit lines, the new Belt Parkway makes them readily accessible by automobile. The new Cross Bay Parkway Bridge and Boulevard connecting Rockaway Beach to the Belt Parkway eliminates a bottleneck that has been notorious for some years.

Another important addition to the city's park system is the large area on the north shore of Jamaica Bay at the Spring Creek Basin acquired in conjunction with the development of the Belt Parkway. With the eventual cleaning up of the waters of Jamaica Bay this area is destined to become one of the city's great waterfront parks providing recreation, boating and safe bathing.

Although The Bronx has always had a larger percentage of its area in parks than any other borough, practically all of this has been in its northerly portion. The southern and the most populous half has been lacking in local park and recreational facilities. It is highly significant to record the acquisition of Soundview and Ferry Point parks.

Soundview Park of about 93 acres is located on the north shore of the Bronx River where it meets the East River. Ferry Point Park was acquired in connection with the building of the Whitestone Bridge; it is a peninsula of about 171 acres and accommodates the northern anchorage of the bridge.

In Richmond some land was acquired for a proposed cross-county parkway. Development of Marine Park, destined to be another of the city's great waterfront parks, has been started by dredging and filling, but much remains to be done. (See picture, page 12.)

In 1939 the Association, together with twenty other civic organizations, was much concerned over a proposal of the Triborough Bridge Authority to use a large part of historical Battery Park, Manhattan, as an approach for a high-level bridge between Manhattan and Brooklyn and opposed the project at the public hearings held thereon by city and Federal agencies. The final decision to substitute a tunnel for a bridge has prevented what would have been an unnecessary invasion and spoilation of park property. In connection with the construction of the tunnel and its approaches and the proposed rebuilding of Battery Park by the Park Department, there are still to be solved certain problems regarding public rights in this area and the preservation of historic landmarks.

SOME PROBLEMS AFFECTING THE PARK SYSTEM

While most of the discussion of progress on features of the regional structure which have a bearing on parks will be treated in other Bulletins, three problems are so intimately related to parks that a brief discussion of them is included here. These are water pollution, transportation and neighborhood planning.

Water Pollution

In summer the most used facilities of the park system are the beaches. The hordes of people who swarm to Coney Island, Jacob Riis Park, Rockaway Beach, Jones Beach, Orchard Beach, Rye Beach and the Atlantic oceanfront in New Jersey, are evidence of this popularity. The development of natural swimming facilities nearer the population centers is not now practicable because of the sewage pollution in the waters of the Port of New York. Even some of the above-named beaches are sub-standard in the degree of purity required for safe bathing.[1]

The progress made in the improvement of these beaches is remarkable but the job will not be done until the sewage problem is solved. Every day New York City discharges a billion gallons of sewage into the waters surrounding the city; only about a third of this receives any treatment whatever. Farther up the Hudson the river-bank towns continue to pour their sewage into the river. The New Jersey waterfront communities are notorious in this respect. The Interstate Sanitation Commission on the 4th of August, 1941, issued its first compulsory order requiring the City of Elizabeth, N. J., to start treating about half of its sewage by September 1, 1941 and comply with the terms of the Tri-State Compact by September, 1943. Sewage disposal, as the City Planning Commission has pointed out[2] is largely a matter of financing programs already worked out. Those who are interested in the development of parks should not overlook the fact that funds provided for sewage disposal plants will make possible the development of important and needed recreational facilities.

Transportation

Parks of more than neighborhood significance require for their complete usefulness the travel of con-

siderable distance to and from them. Transportation thus is an essential part of a regional park system. Parkways and highways make outlying parks and beaches readily available to automobile owners but the improvement of forms of mass transportation should be a concern of park officials. Some of the problems are indicated by the following examples.

On any Sunday in the season an investigator will find at the Pelham Bay Park station of the Interborough a double file of passengers a block long or more, waiting for a bus to take them to Orchard Beach. To get to Jones Beach by way of the Long Island Railroad and the connecting bus line is an arduous and comparatively expensive trip. A waiting line, like the one at Pelham Bay, may be seen at the end of the subway line at Nostrand and Flatbush avenues in Brooklyn on hot Sunday mornings waiting for the Green Line Bus to Jacob Riis Park.

The pollution of the central waters of the Region which has made it necessary to locate beaches in outlying districts, has indirectly placed a burden on transportation. Another factor in this abnormal load on transportation is the fact that adequate local recreational facilities including neighborhood parks are lacking in many congested areas, requiring people to pack up and go to remote places on holidays if they are to get any open air recreation.

Neighborhood Planning

The definite location of each small park and playground required to serve the needs of the densely settled areas of the Region is a local rather than a regional problem. The provision for such facilities in sufficient quantity as an element in a well developed residential neighborhood is, however, a problem of regional importance. Lack of neighborhood parks is an important cause of urban blight, as the owner of land in any central slum area will readily admit.

The Federal Housing Administration recognizes the need for park acreage in new developments both in its subdivision standards and its financial rating of neighborhoods. Yet new developments in outlying areas of the Region are now in the process of construction without provision for adequate park space.[1] Experience to date indicates that the municipality is generally more reluctant to develop and maintain neighborhood parks than the subdivider to provide sufficient acreage. To meet this difficulty the Federal Housing Administration has provided, in some instances, for a reservation by covenant of a part of subdivided land for park purposes which will be available in the future to the

[1] See report of Ekroth Laboratories, Inc., published in the *New York World Telegram*, June 30, 1941.

[2] See "Adoption of Sewage Treatment Plant Sites and Tributary Areas and of a City-Wide Map Thereof as a Part of the Master Plan," New York City Planning Commission, April 16, 1941.

[1] See Information Bulletin No. 46, "Defects of Existing Subdivisions Suggest Need for More Effective Control," September 18, 1939.

municipality without cost. The reluctance on the part of municipalities to take areas needed for parks from the tax rolls or to take on park maintenance is penny-wise and shortsighted.

Neighborhood parks do more than provide recreation. They stabilize land values in residential areas. Recognition of this fact is to be found in the language of the New York Urban Redevelopment Corporations Law which requires of each redevelopment plan that it provide for "public facilities, including, but not limited to, school, fire, police, transportation, *park, playground and recreation*" (italics added). Some of the expanding suburbs of today are in serious danger of becoming tomorrow's blighted areas because of the same lack of intelligent provision for neighborhood parks which was characteristic of the nineteenth century development of the Region's central areas.

PARKWAY SYSTEM

The term "parkway" has been used to designate quite different types of parks and highways, but is now generally limited to the type of express route for passenger vehicles that has been extensively developed under that name in those parts of the Region east of the Hudson River. The pioneer route of this character was the Bronx River Parkway.

The Graphic Regional Plan contemplated and proposed a region-wide system of such parkways comparable to that which had by 1928 been adopted and partly constructed by the Westchester County Park Commission. Parkways were planned to play an important part in both the recreational and the highway systems of the Region. In this Bulletin they are discussed primarily from the former viewpoint, that is, as connecting residential centers with outlying public

and private recreational areas lying along the waterfronts and water courses, on the hills and lakes, or forming other natural scenic features. In addition, they include within themselves facilities for picnicking, hiking, horseback riding and other more active forms of recreation.

As a result of their efficiency for carrying vehicles rapidly and in pleasant surroundings—way beyond the efficiency of the ordinary highway passing through a series of urban centers—the importance of parkways for handling part of the normal movement of weekday as well as week-end traffic has increased. The effect of parkway progress on the improvement of the main highway system will, however, be discussed more fully in a later Bulletin.

Action on 1937 Program

Any progress in developing a regional parkway system involves a series of steps. First must come public demand backed by a willingness to support the necessary appropriations; next must follow official preparation and adoption of a general plan and the acquisition of the necessary rights-of-way; finally the adoption of detailed plans and construction. There is often a considerable interval of time between these steps.

In connection with its previous reports, the Regional Plan Association has made recommendations for carrying out certain of these steps to advance further links in the regional system. The last such program was presented in 1937,[1] and a summary of these recommendations and the action taken to date is given below. There was action on 12 of the 14 projects; in six cases they were carried to or beyond the stage recommended.

[1] Information Bulletin No. 39, "Important Projects in the Region Needing Immediate Attention," December 6, 1937; also FROM PLAN TO REALITY, Two (1938), Chapter VI.

Project	*1937 Recommendation*	*Action to Date*
Southern Parkway in Queens	Construction	Completed
Brooklyn Circumferential Parkway	Construction	Completed
Extension of Bronx River and Mosholu Parkways	Construction	Maps adopted and lands acquired
Eastern State Parkway	Construction	Completed in Region
East River Drive, Manhattan	Construction	Complete except for two short links
Southern State Parkway	Construction	Extended into Suffolk County
Passaic River Parkway	Construction	Adopted on Master Plan of Bergen County
Merritt Parkway Extension	Construction	Completed in Region
Harlem River Drive, Manhattan	Adoption and mapping	Adopted and preliminary studies made by Borough President
Shore Parkway in New Jersey	Mapping and acquisition	No action
Saddle River Parkway	Mapping and acquisition	Adopted on Master Plan of Bergen County as a ribbon park
Parkway connecting Watchung and South Mountain Reservations	Adoption and mapping	Studied by New Jersey State Chamber of Commerce
Mohansic-Norwalk Parkway	Adoption and acquisition	No action
Upper Hackensack River Parkway	Adoption and acquisition	Adopted on Master Plan of Bergen County

A Review of Progress

What has been accomplished in acquisition of parkway rights-of-way since 1928 is illustrated in Figure 2, which has already been described. A graphic picture of the twelve-year progress in the completion of parkways as passenger car routes is presented in Figure 3.

The striking feature of this map is the complete concentration of such routes in New York City and those suburban areas lying east of the Hudson River. In thin full lines are shown those comparatively few parkways which existed in 1928, and in thin broken lines a few express connections, existing or authorized, which will complete a circulatory system within the City of New York. The total mileage of parkways existing or under construction in the Region is now 306 as compared with 41 miles at the end of 1928. The advances of the last four years are described below.

In New York.—The outstanding parkway development in the New York State part of the Region since 1936 has been the extension into and through New York City of the Long Island and Westchester parkways, accomplished mainly under the direction of Robert Moses as Park Commissioner and Chairman of the various Authorities under which important links

were planned and constructed. Credit should also be given to Borough President Stanley M. Isaacs of Manhattan who has been responsible for the East River Drive in that borough. Except for certain important missing links, broad parkways, including many new recreational features, now encircle and serve every section of the city.

Among the recent parkway additions completed or under construction are the Belt Parkway around Brooklyn and Queens (some 33 miles in length), the Whitestone Parkway, the East River Drive, and the Henry Hudson, Hutchinson River and Bronx River parkway extensions. An important link in the parkway system, the Whitestone Bridge, was also completed during this period. Now under construction are the Brooklyn-Battery Tunnel and its approaches which will connect the Belt Parkway with the West Side Highway, the Henry Hudson Parkway and the East River Drive. While not classified as a parkway, the West Side Elevated Highway is an important link in the arterial parkway system.

The Henry Hudson Parkway has been extended south along the Hudson River through Riverside Park to connect with the West Side Elevated Highway at

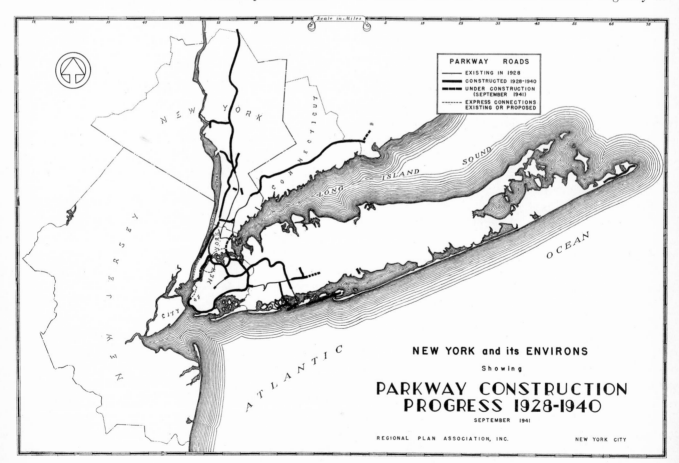

NEW YORK and its ENVIRONS

Showing

PARKWAY CONSTRUCTION PROGRESS 1928-1940

SEPTEMBER 1941

REGIONAL PLAN ASSOCIATION, INC.   NEW YORK CITY

FIGURE 3

72nd Street. At the northern end it connects with a widened Saw Mill River Parkway in Westchester County. On the other side of Manhattan the new East River Drive has been planned along the waterfront from the Battery to the Triborough Bridge and is completed except for the sections between 30th and 49th streets and from Montgomery Street to the Brooklyn-Battery Tunnel. With the completion of these links and the projected Harlem River Drive connecting with the George Washington Bridge and the Henry Hudson Parkway a nearly complete circumferential drive around Manhattan will become a reality.

The most extensive new parkway development in the city is the Belt Parkway extending from Owls Head Park in Brooklyn to the Whitestone Bridge in Queens. Skirting the Brooklyn shore along the Narrows, it swings inland back of the Coney Island peninsula and continues east to Marine Park. It then follows along the north shore of Jamaica Bay, crosses into Queens and joins the Southern Parkway. Near the Nassau County line the parkway swings north via the Laurelton Parkway and continues north as the Cross Island Parkway to the Whitestone Bridge. From the bridge, the Whitestone Parkway approach connects with the Grand Central Parkway at the Flushing Meadow Park. Both the Whitestone Bridge and the Whitestone Parkway were completed in time for the opening in 1939 of the World's Fair on the Flushing Meadow Park site.

Branching off the main belt parkway and crossing it at various points are other parkways of the system. The Long Island parkways extend into Nassau and Suffolk counties from the Cross Island Parkway section of the belt; the Hutchinson River Parkway, through The Bronx and Westchester County, has its southern terminus at the Whitestone Bridge; and the Grand Central Parkway, crossing the Belt Parkway in Alley Pond Park, ties in Manhattan and The Bronx via the Triborough Bridge.

The Hutchinson River Parkway Extension in The Bronx is scheduled for completion in October, 1941. It will connect the present terminus, in Pelham Bay Park, with the Whitestone Bridge. The Bronx River Parkway, now terminating in Bronx Park, will be extended to Eastern Boulevard and Soundview Park.

Some progress was made in acquiring land in Staten Island for the proposed cross-county parkway extending from Goethals Bridge to Marine Park in connection with a new state hospital in the center of the island. The parkway is included in the first step of the master plan for parks by the City Planning Commission.

In Nassau County the Northern State Parkway was extended about three miles to connect with an extension across the county of the Wantagh State Parkway, both being opened in December, 1938. This has greatly improved the connections to Jones Beach from the northern part of Long Island. With the opening of the Hutchinson River Parkway Extension, referred to above, there will be continuous parkway routes to Jones Beach from Bridgeport, Peekskill, or the present terminus of the Eastern State Parkway east of Poughkeepsie. The Southern State Parkway was extended about two miles into Suffolk County, December 16, 1939; a further extension to Belmont Lake State Park is under construction.

In Westchester County a serious bottleneck was eliminated by the completion March 13, 1939, of the Fleetwood Viaduct on the Cross County Parkway. A direct connection of this parkway with the Saw Mill River Parkway, which was widened from that point south to the New York City line, was completed in October, 1940. Ramp connections between the Fleetwood Viaduct and the Bronx River Parkway are under construction as well as a widening of the Hutchinson River Parkway south of Westchester Avenue in the Town of Harrison.

The Eastern State Parkway was extended to Arthursburg in Dutchess County, at the limits of the Region, in November, 1937, but north of the Peekskill Hollow Road it was, except for one small section, only two lanes in width. This has all been increased to four lanes, a final bottleneck through Roaring Brook and Fahnestock state parks being completed in 1939. In 1938 the parkway was extended beyond the Region to Freedom Plains east of Poughkeepsie.

In Connecticut.—The completion of the Merritt Parkway as a four-lane route from the New York State line to the eastern shore of the Housatonic River just outside the Region, with a spur from that point to the Boston Post Road at Milford, has been the outstanding addition during the past four years to the suburban sections of the regional parkway system. The initial and westerly section was opened June 29, 1938, and the entire stretch was completed in September, 1940.

Plans have been adopted for continuing the parkway as the Wilbur Cross Parkway to connect with U. S. Route 20 at a point east of Springfield, Mass. A short section south of the Massachusetts state line has been completed and parts of the remainder are under construction.

New Jersey Lags Behind.—New Jersey has lagged behind New York and Connecticut in the development of parkways and to date there are no completed parkway routes in the New Jersey portion of the Region.

There is, however, a growing appreciation in northern New Jersey of parkways and the benefits which they might bring to the communities therein.

The Highways and Parkways Committee of the New Jersey State Chamber of Commerce made, in 1941, a study of a parkway system for the state which included the Palisades Parkway, the Pleasant Valley Parkway, the Watchung Parkway, the Raritan River Parkway and the Shore Parkway, all of which are shown on the Graphic Regional Plan. This same committee has drafted a proposed Act to provide for the acquisition and development of limited access highways and parkways in the State of New Jersey, to be built by the State Highway Commissioner after designation of such routes by the Legislature.[1] The parkway provisions include the following:

"'Parkway' shall mean a state highway especially designed for fast moving passenger vehicles and with special treatment in landscaping and planting along its borders, which borders may also include recreational features such as pedestrian paths, bridle trails, overlooks and picnic areas."

"Lands needed for parkway purposes are declared to be those required for the travelled way, together with those lands necessary to protect scenic views and to provide overlooks, occasional parking areas and roadside picnic areas."

"The State Highway Commissioner shall have the authority to restrict, either continuously or to specified times, the use of roadways in parkways to passenger vehicles and to otherwise limit the size, type and weight of vehicles using such roadways."

The New Jersey State Planning Board has for sev-

eral years been urging parkway construction in the state and in a report of 1938 stated:

"Now, surely, with the first mad rush of building 'utilitarian' highways over, New Jersey can little afford longer to neglect incorporating in future highway construction the basic safety and scenic values of parkway design."[1]

Since then they have been making studies for a system of scenic routes tied in with a comprehensive plan of public recreational facilities.

A special committee appointed by the House of Assembly to study the method of constructing and financing state parkways and highways on a self-liquidating basis published a report March 31, 1941. The committee recommended consideration of the establishment of a New Jersey State Parkway Authority to plan, finance and construct, without pledging the credit of the State, a system of toll parkways and highways to connect state and county parks, and mountain and beach resorts, with the large metropolitan districts.

One item of construction that should be mentioned is the extension, opened August 12, 1940, of the Hendrick Hudson Drive along the foot of the Palisades from the Englewood-Dyckman Street Ferry Plaza south to River Road in Edgewater. Classified as a secondary parkway on the Regional Plan, this is essentially an access road to the Palisades Interstate Park and therefore is not shown in Figure 3.

---

[1] "How Municipalities Can Aid in Roadside Control Along State Highways," New Jersey State Chamber of Commerce, December, 1940, page 16.

[1] "Where Shall We Play—a Report on the Outdoor Recreational Needs of New Jersey," New Jersey State Planning Board, 1938, page 27.

Courtesy, Department of Parks, City of New York

Marine Park, Staten Island
The peninsula was recently formed by hydraulic fill.

The inclusion of five parkway routes in the Master Plan for Bergen County adopted by the County Planning Board on October 23, 1940, represents the first step toward official approval of such routes in that county.

AN IMMEDIATE AND POST-WAR PROGRAM

For more than a year this country has concentrated on transforming itself from a Nation at peace to the arsenal of world democracy. At current rates of defense spending, indications are that a large percentage of the Nation's annual income may be spent for defense purposes. Obviously defense efforts will detract from non-military public works. On first thought this would suggest a greatly curtailed park development program in every part of the Nation.

Abandonment of park and parkway development for the duration of the war would, however, be as short-sighted as neglect of the recreational facilities at army posts or failure to eliminate highway bottlenecks at military reservations. Parks play a vital part in the maintenance of civilian health and morale and parkways are essential links in the regional highway system as well as invaluable transport arteries for emergency military use.

Post-war employment problems created by a shift from all-out production for defense to a program of normal activities require advance planning and organization for action. The Association has made a careful analysis of recreational needs of the Region and formulated a program for advocating specific projects of the regional park and parkway system which will be needed in the more immediate future. The greater part of the program is designed to take up slack which will follow peak defense spending. Several projects for which there is demonstrable defense need are recommended for immediate development, some have been selected to correct present deficiencies in recreational facilities and others are proposed for initiation in advance of acute needs. Recommended action on these varies from official adoption and mapping of proposals to acquisition of necessary lands and their development.

The program outlined in the following pages has been carefully considered in the light of current conditions and with the following principles in mind.

1. If land has been reserved and plans made, post-war development can proceed immediately. Such a policy will not detract from the national defense effort and will supply a reservoir of well-conceived projects to meet unemployment problems following the war.
2. Existing parks should not be used for military purposes except in the event of acute emergency.
3. Maintenance of already developed parks and parkways is of first importance. Development at the expense of maintenance produces a questionable net improvement.

4. While this program does not include specific recommendations regarding local or neighborhood parks the need for these in both blighted and newly developing areas cannot be emphasized too much. Building development interests at the present time still are inclined to ignore such amenities as parks and play areas upon which the real value of the neighborhood must in the long run depend.

As pointed out elsewhere in this report, the greatest need for recreational facilities is west of the Hudson River and especially in northern New Jersey. The proposals outlined for this sector of the Region are no more elaborate than have already been realized in other parts of the Region but are of such extent that they can be achieved only through a program covering a period of years.

The location of projects included in this program is shown in Figure 4 on page 14. Recommended action on each proposal is given on the list just below the map; the projects are described separately below under the headings of parks and parkways.

Parks

Recreational needs of the Region can be divided into two general types. The first includes local or neighborhood facilities which are primarily of community interest; and the second is made up of the larger parks or reservations, the benefits of which may be enjoyed by all persons living in the Region, provided they are accessible at a reasonable cost for transportation.

A four-year program for advancing projects of the latter scope is presented as a broad-scale guide to recreational problems of the immediate future. Adherence to the program will make the execution of each project count as a step toward the ultimate realization of a comprehensive system of recreational lands rather than dissociated or unrelated objectives of numerous communities.

1. *Waterfront, Monmouth County*

In considering the opportunities for public recreation in New Jersey it is appropriate to begin with its shorefront. The need for waterfront parks has been generally recognized for a long time. The sites illustrated on the map in Figure 4 are located at Union Beach, Sea Bright, Sandy Hook and Sea Girt. Repeated efforts have been made to persuade the War Department to assign a portion of Sandy Hook Reservation for public use and likewise various attempts to obtain the use of the State Militia Reservation at Sea Girt have been made. These sites contain practically the only sections of undeveloped beachfronts along the coast and were selected because acquisition of comparable sites within this area would be prohibitive.

Two alternative sites for an oceanfront park at Sea Bright have been proposed, one by the Sea Bright Park Commission and the other by the Board of Commerce and Navigation. The site at Union Beach was also proposed by the New Jersey Board of Commerce and Navigation. Both of the sites are well located with respect to the population they will serve and should be acquired before improved means of access are provided.

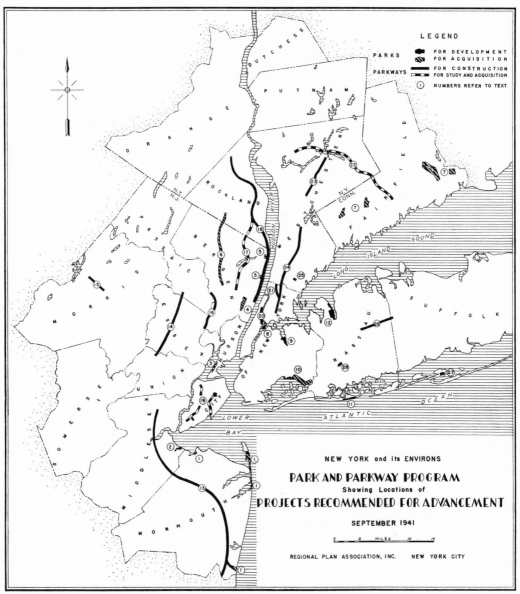

FIGURE 4

Recommended Action: A—Construction or development (as priorities permit); B—Acquisition; C—Adoption and mapping

Key No.	Project	Action	Key No.	Project	Action	Key No.	Project	Action
	PARKS		10.	North Shore, Jamaica Bay........	B	19.	Staten Island	B & C
1.	Waterfront, Monmouth County....	B	11.	Oceanfront, Nassau County.......	A	20.	Harlem River Drive..............	A
2.	Cheesequake Park Extension......	A & B	12.	Hempstead Harbor, Nassau County.	A	21.	Mosholu	A
3.	Newark Bay Waterfront..........	B				22.	Mohansic-Norwalk	B & C
4.	Overpeck Meadows	B		PARKWAYS		23.	Saw Mill River...................	A
5.	Areas along top of Palisades.......	B & C	13.	To New Jersey Shore.............	A	24.	Bronx River	A
6.	Saddle River	B	14.	Pleasant Valley	A	25.	Cross County	A
7.	Along Merritt Parkway...........	B	15.	Lake Hopatcong	A	26.	Northern State	A
8.	Wards Island	A	16.	Passaic River	A	27.	Ocean	A
9.	Flushing Meadow	A	17.	Upper Hackensack	B & C	28.	Southern State	A
			18.	Palisades	A			

2. *Extension to Cheesequake Park*

The extension of this state park area in Middlesex County to the waterfront would greatly increase its usefulness. The development of the new section could proceed gradually, installation of bathing facilities being dependent on purification of the adjoining waters.

3. *Newark Bay Waterfront*

Although a plan for the extension of existing park areas along Newark Bay was adopted by the Bayonne City Planning Commission some time ago, nothing more has been done to advance this project. The necessary underwater land should be acquired by the city as a step toward the rehabilitation of that section of the New Jersey waterfront.

4. *Overpeck Meadows*

This proposal was outlined and listed for acquisition in the previous future program. Its need and value is still apparent. The section of New Jersey that it would serve presents a particularly difficult problem in supplying recreational facilities in that the surrounding areas are all intensively urbanized. The execution of this proposal would make up in part for the lack of park areas in nearby communities.

The project has been advanced from its former status in that it has been adopted by the Bergen County Planning Board as part of its Master Plan, referred to on page 5.

5. *Areas Along Top of Palisades*

During the past four years additional property has been acquired by the Palisades Interstate Park Commission so that they now own all but 15 per cent of the land necessary to preserve the Palisades and provide an adequate right-of-way for a parkway leading north from the George Washington Bridge. Practically all of the land up to the New Jersey state line has been received in gifts by tracts from members of the Rockefeller family. It is urgent that the remainder of this be acquired and plans for a roadway adopted as a link in the proposed parkway approach to Bear Mountain Park described under project No. 18.

6. *Saddle River*

This proposal was listed for mapping and acquisition in the program issued four years ago. The section in Bergen County has been adopted on the county Master Plan. It is recommended that needed land be acquired before it is lost to other uses. Much of the land might be obtained by dedication since the adjoining property would be greatly benefited.

7. *Along Merritt Parkway*

As outlined in the previous program of public improvements for the part of Fairfield County in the Region, strategic areas along the Merritt Parkway should be under public ownership for recreational use. The urgency of this proposal lies in the fact that these areas should be obtained before development makes acquisition prohibitive.

8. *Wards Island*

Recreational facilities in this section of the city are badly needed to serve the needs of the densely populated sections of the upper east side of Manhattan and the lower Bronx. The potentialities of Wards Island afford an excellent opportunity to fulfill this need. Plans for development of this proposal have been completed by the New York City Park Department and include a foot bridge across the river at East 103rd Street. Advancement has been deferred because of insufficient funds to transfer patients of the island's institutions elsewhere. This would involve an appropriation by the State Legislature and it is hoped that means can be found to accomplish this.

An alternative to the foot bridge is worthy of consideration and is shown on the Graphic Regional Plan. It consists of a highway and pedestrian bridge from Wards Island to the vicinity of 106th Street which would connect by means of a parkway with the roads of Central Park.

9. *Flushing Meadow Park*

The closing of the World's Fair in October, 1940, made available 1,255 acres for a city park. Development plans made by the New York City Park Department make provision for every type of passive and active recreation. When completed it will contain more extensive facilities than any other park in the city. Among these are bicycle paths, bridle trails, pedestrian walks, baseball diamonds, a boat basin, and marginal neighborhood playgrounds. Periodic appropriation of funds should be allocated to this project so that work can be progressively advanced.

10. *North Shore of Jamaica Bay*

This area extends and rounds out existing park areas along the north shore of Jamaica Bay from Old Mill Creek to the Head of the Bay. Purification of the now polluted water is assured in the city's plans for completing the construction in 1943 of new sewage disposal plants surrounding Jamaica Bay. Following this such recreational pursuits as bathing, fishing and

many others will be possible along this stretch of the city's waterfront. Land should be acquired in the near future so that physical improvement can proceed with the clearing up of pollution. Much of this land should be preserved in its natural state.

11, 12. *Waterfront Parks, Nassau County*

These proposals call for an extension to the Town of Hempstead Park at Point Lookout and acquisition of a park site on the west shore of Hempstead Harbor in the Town of North Hempstead. The existing town park at Point Lookout is of insufficient size to accommodate the need of local residents. An unusual opportunity exists to expand this park westerly along the only remaining undeveloped stretch of oceanfront on the Long Beach peninsula.

In the Town of North Hempstead the provision of public open space has not kept pace with its rapid urbanization. During the past decade this section of Nassau County experienced a greater rate of population increase than any similar area in the New York Region. The problem of making provision for the recreational needs of the area should be faced now. Abandonment of the sand pits on the site proposed is only a matter of time. Parts of the site should be acquired for park purposes within the near future and with the view of progressive acquisition of the remainder.

Parkways

Of the 16 parkway projects that have been compiled for consideration in the immediate future, most are in the New Jersey sector of the Region. Since the early twenties New Jersey has concentrated on supplying the needs of utilitarian traffic and has permitted a great lag of equally important recreational services. It follows that an increasing share of public revenues should now be urged for development of facilities for recreational traffic.

The present extent of parkway routes in the eastern sector of the Region, shown in Figure 3, will at some future time be supplemented by at least 116 additional miles. Rights-of-way for these have been acquired at various times[1] during the past twelve years. The planned pattern for these can be picked out by comparing the above illustration with Figure 2. As part of this long range program to supply recreational traffic arteries, officials of New York State have instituted a bill which will divert funds from unexpended railroad grade crossing elimination bonds for construction or reconstruction of parkway links in various parts of the State. Both branches of the State Legislature have approved the measure and final decision will be made by popular referendum in the fall election of 1941.

Six out of ten items of the Association's immediate parkway program for the New York sector of the Region are part of the contemplated plan of the State. A description of the complete program follows:

13. *To New Jersey Shore Resorts*

One of the most serious traffic problems in New Jersey is the lack of a modern traffic artery to the shore resorts. On many oc-

---

[1] See FROM PLAN TO REALITY (1933), page 51, and FROM PLAN TO REALITY, Two (1938), page III-2.

casions during the summer thousands of cars are backed up for miles due to interruptions from cross traffic. There is little need to discuss the usefulness and advantages of a parkway route since the benefits of Westchester County and Long Island parkways are so well known.

This project would extend from State Highway No. 25 at Rahway, in a general southeasterly direction to and parallel to the oceanfront in Monmouth County. Studies by the Highways and Parkways Committee, New Jersey State Chamber of Commerce, propose to extend the route south to serve Atlantic City. The project is regarded as the outstanding opportunity for the beginning of a state system of parks and parkways in New Jersey.

14. *Pleasant Valley*

This proposal extends southerly from New Jersey State Highway No. 6 at Great Notch along the valley between First and Second Watchung Mountains passing through the South Mountain Reservation to a point south of Route S-24 in Springfield. From here it is proposed to extend the route south with a freeway type of route to connect with the Shore Parkway at Rahway. Details of this will be presented in a later Bulletin dealing with highways.

15. *Lake Hopatcong*

This project would provide a vitally needed highway approach to the Picatinny Arsenal which not only would serve an immediate defense need but will have a post-war value as a link in the proposed system of parkways for the Region. The proposed link is approximately five miles long, running from Rockaway to the Arsenal Reservation. It has the complete backing of the Morris County Planning Board. The completion of this project is urgently needed as it offers a logical solution for the relief of present traffic congestion.

16. *Passaic River*

A parkway is proposed to extend from the mouth of Second River in Essex County to New Jersey State Highway No. 3 in Paterson. This project was listed for construction in the previous program of urgent projects. Its present status is the same as formerly indicated except that the portion in Bergen County has been adopted as part of the county Master Plan.

17. *Upper Hackensack*

This project runs north from New Jersey State Highway No. 4 to tie in with the proposed Palisades Parkway (Project 18) at West Nyack. It will supply a much needed northerly traffic outlet and is regarded as an outstanding opportunity for parkway development west of the Hudson River. As the Hackensack River above Oradel is an important source of water supply, recreational use of its banks should be limited by such restriction as the water supply and health authorities would require. The proposal should be officially adopted and a start made on acquiring its right-of-way.

18. *Palisades*

This proposal will provide a parkway route from the George Washington Bridge to Bear Mountain Reservation. A quicker and safer approach road to this recreational area is needed to provide for the increasing numbers seeking to use the park. Construction of this proposal will relieve congestion along the section of Route 9-W that it parallels and it will supply a badly needed modern traffic artery west of the Hudson River.

19. *Staten Island*

Any comprehensive program for the future development of Richmond should include the construction of parkways. The problem of acquiring necessary land should be faced within the immediate future. The proposals shown on Figure 4 call for a northerly extension of Willow Brook Parkway to the Goethals Bridge and a southerly extension of same to Marine Park. Another route runs from the plaza of the contemplated Narrows Crossing to the Outerbridge Crossing with a spur to Wolf's Pond Park.

20. *Harlem River Drive*

The project provides a connection between the north end of East River Drive and the tunnel under West 178th Street connecting with the George Washington Bridge. Playfields and promenades developed along its borders will make this proposal a definite neighborhood asset and construction of the roadway will provide a much needed northerly outlet for East River Drive and Triborough Bridge traffic. Final plans should be adopted and the proposal completed within the next four years. The adjacent areas should be rezoned to promote a proper type of private development.

21. *Mosholu*

This proposal would supply a modern traffic connection between the Bronx River and Henry Hudson parkways. Final plans have already been adopted for its reconstruction and completion should be scheduled with that of the southerly extension of Bronx River Parkway.

22. *Mohansic-Norwalk*

A circumferential parkway should ultimately be constructed from the Merritt Parkway at Norwalk to connect at Mohansic Park with the Bronx Parkway Extension. This proposal was listed in the previous program of the Association and it is still regarded as a worthwhile project. Much of the route would utilize New York City watershed property in Westchester County. A plan should be adopted and a start made on acquisition of the remainder of necessary right-of-way.

23, 24, 25. *Westchester and The Bronx*

Extension of Saw Mill River Parkway from Chappaqua north to Katonah to join New York State Highway 132; straightening and rebuilding Bronx River Parkway from Kensico Dam to the city line; a southerly extension of the latter to Eastern Boulevard involving relocation of existing roadway and a new link south of Bronx Park; and a direct connection from Cross County Parkway to Hutchinson River Parkway are projects listed for development under the State's plan to use unexpended railroad grade-crossing elimination funds for highway purposes.

26, 27, 28. *Long Island*

The following proposals included in the Association's program for the immediate future are also part of the State's program outlined above: extension of Northern State Parkway from Union Avenue in Westbury to State Highway No. 110 in South Huntington; a cut-off on Southern State Parkway across the north end of Hempstead Lake State Park; and a short extension of Ocean Parkway to the boat basin at Cap Tree State Park.

Whitestone Bridge Connecting The Bronx and Queens—a Major Link in the Metropolitan Loop Highway

III. GENERAL TRAFFIC HIGHWAYS

The most noticeable change that would strike a visitor who is familiar with the New York Region but who has been absent thirteen years is the extent to which the highway system has been improved. He might be astonished at the amount accomplished but he would have little occasion to wonder at the pattern of routes if he remembered the system of highways proposed by the Regional Plan of New York and Its Environs. Expanding and modernizing the highway system at all levels of government—Federal, interstate, state, county and municipal — is the outstanding achievement in regional development, credit for which is due the officials and staff members of the various highway agencies.

In its preceding Bulletin[1] the Regional Plan Association discussed parkway progress and a future parkway program was presented as part of the regional recreational system. This report reviews in a similar manner the growth of the highways available for all types of traffic, showing how the parkway system fits into and supplements the general pattern. A special section is devoted to expressways, including a proposed regional system of such routes, part of which would be open to general traffic and part of which would continue to be restricted to light passenger vehicles. A program for the future, particularly as part of a post-war public works program, is presented.

Striking Advances Made

The Graphic Regional Plan published in 1929 showed a system of major highway routes, existing and proposed, involving a total of 2,548 miles.[2] Some

additions have since been made in the process of keeping the Plan up-to-date. Progress is reported during the twelve-year period ending with 1940 on 1,419 miles of major routes representing about 54 per cent of the mileage in the original scheme. A large part of this, 979 miles, involved construction of new routes or the substantial improvement of old ones, so increasing their capacity that they could take their proper place in the regional system. The balance of the progress consists in the official adoption or study of certain routes assuring their future construction.

In the central part of the Region the adoption on January 2, 1941, by the City Planning Commission of New York City of a "Master Plan of Express Highways, Parkways and Major Streets" has assured a proper coordination into and through New York City of previously isolated expressways. It has also given impetus to the theory, long advanced by the Association, that a considerable part of such routes should be available for general traffic, giving commercial vehicles the same opportunities for express movement as has been so well supplied for passenger vehicles in Westchester, Putnam, Dutchess and Fairfield counties and on Long Island. It will be shown herein how completely this Master Plan for New York City highways ties in with the proposed regional highway system.

There has been a greatly increased recognition of the need of establishing some adequate form of roadside control in order that state and county highways may continue to have an efficiency which, in many cases, has proved only temporary as uncontrolled roadside development has brought congestion and increased accident hazard. The New Jersey State Chamber of Commerce and the New York and New Jersey Roadside Councils have been particularly active in pointing out the urgency of this problem and in advocating measures to solve it.

---

[1] References to the "preceding Bulletin" throughout this chapter refer to the preceding chapter of this Report.

[2] The Plan also contained subordinate highway routes made up of about 1,800 miles of minor regional highways and 2,000 miles of important connecting routes. Progress on these is not reported herein except where small sections of the former have since been re-classified as major routes.

The following pages review briefly the progress on the major regional routes in the twelve years from 1928 through 1940, with emphasis on the last four years of that period and with notes on new developments in 1941. These are grouped according to their place in a diagrammatic scheme made up of circumferential, inner and radial routes. A second section deals with expressways and a final one presents a four-year program for the advancement of the high-

A summary of the mileages of major improvements for both the twelve-year and concluding four-year periods are given in the table facing page 4. In many cases routes previously improved have been further improved since 1936, as reported herein, but the mileage involved is not included in the 1936-1940 figures.

CIRCUMFERENTIAL ROUTES

The system of circumferential routes consists of a

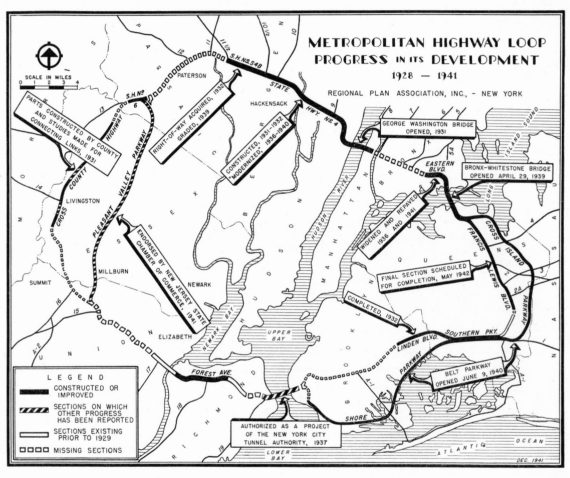

FIGURE 1

way system available for general traffic.[1] As in the parkway program presented in the preceding Bulletin, the proposals herein will, of course, be subject in many cases to Federal priorities resulting from the national defense program and most of them will, therefore, logically fall into a post-war program of public works. Wherever possible preliminary studies should be made and necessary rights-of-way acquired so as to facilitate their inclusion in such a deferred program.

series of concentric rings about the central core of the Region to provide circulation generally at right angles to radial arteries. The Metropolitan Loop is the principal circumferential or belt highway. Progress on the advancement of circumferential routes during the past twelve years may be seen in Figure 2 (facing page 4) and development during the past four years is as follows:

Metropolitan Loop

This route forms the main key of the regional highway system, encircling the intensively urbanized sec-

[1] See FROM PLAN TO REALITY (1933), Chapter II, and FROM PLAN TO REALITY, TWO (1938), Chapters II and III, published by Regional Plan Association, Inc., for a detailed analysis of the periods 1928-1932 and 1933-1936 respectively.

tions of New York and New Jersey at approximately 14 miles from New York City Hall. Its major purpose is to provide through mixed traffic with a central area bypass and a convenient means of interchange between radial routes, thereby relieving congestion within the heart of the Region. Radial arteries connect at the Loop with a system of "Inner Routes" designed to serve the central area.

During the past four years the Brooklyn-Queens segment of the Loop has been paralleled with a parkway. In New Jersey a proposal very similar to this, calling for a 14-mile Pleasant Valley Parkway, has been initiated by the New Jersey State Chamber of Commerce. While both of these will be limited to light

The relation between the present status of the Loop and the advancement of other major highways of the regional system in the central part of the Region is given in Figure 3 (facing page 8).

Excluding the parallel parkways, progress on the main Loop to date shows 48 miles, or 41 per cent, of its total length constructed and an additional 15 miles, or 13 per cent, having received official preliminary action. Of this total, seven miles have been advanced within the past four years. Statistics summarizing progress of the extensions of the Loop are included in those given in the summary table facing page 4.

Major Waterway Crossings.—When the Regional Plan was first published, the only existing major waterway crossing in

Courtesy, Department of Parks, City of New York

METROPOLITAN HIGHWAY LOOP IN THE BOROUGH OF QUEENS
Southern Parkway along the old Conduit right-of-way. Flanking service roads are inadequate
for rapid movement of commercial traffic which is prohibited on the central roadways.

passenger vehicles, they will do much to relieve congestion within the central part of the Region. The Association regards them as important supplements to its original Metropolitan Loop proposal, but still holds that the ultimate development of the latter will require a complete loop available for mixed traffic.

A simplified diagram of the Loop, indicating the present character and extent of progress toward its development since the preparation of the Graphic Plan in 1928, is given in Figure 1. Progress shown along its mixed traffic course does not necessarily imply that in each case an adequate type of route has been supplied.

the course of the Loop was the Goethals Bridge over the Arthur Kill, which provided the southerly connecting link between New York and New Jersey. In 1931 the George Washington Bridge supplied the northern interstate connection. The third major waterway was crossed by the Whitestone Bridge which opened April 29, 1939. Ultimately, the proposed Narrows Tunnel and a new bridge over the Harlem River at West 178th Street will be required, each of which has received official consideration.

In New York City.—In Manhattan, the Loop was extended easterly about half a mile from the George Washington Bridge Plaza by a crosstown vehicular tunnel, the first in the city. Constructed by the Port of New York Authority and officially opened June 27, 1940, it is two lanes wide and extends under West 178th Street to connect with the Harlem River Driveway in Highbridge Park. A similar tube is planned under West 179th Street. From the above point the Regional Plan calls for a new bridge over the Harlem River to The Bronx which should include in its design accommodations for future rail communication.

From the Harlem River a new route is proposed to extend across The Bronx to connect and follow Eastern Boulevard from a point where the latter intersects the projected extension of Bronx River Parkway, to and along the Whitestone Bridge into Queens. The section utilizing Eastern Boulevard was widened and repaved in July, 1936, as an approach to the Triborough Bridge; further widening was under way in 1941.

During the past four years advancement of the Queens part of the Loop has taken place section by section so that at the present time a link only about one and a half miles in length through Cunningham Park remains incomplete.[1] On November 13, 1939, a four-mile stretch of Francis Lewis Boulevard[2] from the Whitestone Bridge to the World's Fair Boulevard was opened. Plans call for eventual grade separations at Northern and World's Fair boulevards, Crocheron Avenue, and Union Turnpike. Sufficient land was acquired at these points to permit construction of bridges and ramps. Another portion, from a point south of Grand Central Parkway to Springfield Boulevard, was repaved since the last report of progress, with two 36-foot roadways separated by a five-foot mall.

From the intersection of Springfield Boulevard and Sunrise Highway[3] the route extends westerly through Brooklyn to the proposed Narrows Tunnel. Originally laid out to follow existing and mapped streets, recent study by both the Regional Plan Association and the New York City Planning Commission resulted in realigning the location slightly to the north to follow Linden Boulevard, the Bay Ridge Division of the Long Island Railroad and Fort Hamilton Parkway to the proposed tunnel. The older alignment is retained as a supplementary major route.

In New Jersey.—Occupying the unique position as "gateway" to the Port of New York, New Jersey has concentrated its efforts on the development of arterial trunk line highways converging on river crossings. The merging of through traffic in the northeast counties of the State seriously impedes the movement of local traffic. Congestion along north-south routes can be relieved to a large extent by an adequate bypass around the highly developed and densely populated section.

The New Jersey State Chamber of Commerce appointed a Highways and Parkways Committee to study the problem. One of the chief difficulties confronting them was the location of a modern north-south route to connect the populous northern area with the shore resorts. Their study which was made in 1941, includes a parallel parkway for the entire length of the north-south segment of the Loop in Essex County. This is shown in Figure 1, but is not recorded as progress as defined in this report.

Also, in Bergen County the channelization of New Jersey State Highway No. 4 between Fort Lee and State Highway No. 2 and a grade separation at Maywood Avenue constitute a decided improvement in this segment of the Loop.

A section of the Loop following projected New Jersey State Highway No. S-4B between Arcola and Radburn in Bergen County has been graded. The joint effort by communities through which it passes to develop this in accordance with good standards is described under Radial Route 11½.

Branch of Metropolitan Loop Around Jamaica Bay (Route A-1).—This provides access from the east and west to the resorts of the Rockaway Peninsula connecting with the Metropolitan Loop at Springfield in Queens and via Flatbush Avenue in Brooklyn.

Construction of the Marine Parkway Bridge and its approach road through Jacob Riis Park to connect with Rockaway Beach Boulevard was well under way at the time of the previous report of progress. These have been completed and were formally opened by the Marine Parkway Authority[1] on July 3, 1937.

In July, 1938, a section of the route between the Marine Parkway Bridge approach and Beach 116th Street was completed. This improvement extends the route more than two miles along the north shore of the Rockaway Peninsula and consists of a dual roadway with a central separator strip.

As part of the State's program for eliminating grade crossings on the Rockaway Peninsula, an entirely new route has been supplied[2] between Beach 108th Street and Beach 83rd Street. While this was not included in the original proposals of the Graphic Regional Plan it is regarded as a valuable addition in that it will provide traffic relief in a badly congested section of the city.

Another section of this route which utilizes Rockaway Boulevard from West Broadway in Lawrence to a proposed cut-off to Springfield Boulevard in Queens County was widened and repaved during 1938.

Outer Circumferential Routes

The function of the outer circumferential routes is to connect the principal radial highways and provide direct routes for intersectional travel. The Metropolitan Bypass provides a route around the central area for traffic from or to points outside the Region.

Suburban Belt Highway (Route B).—The most extensive development along the entire route is the Thomas A. Edison Memorial Bridge in Middlesex County which carries the route over the Raritan River. Radial Route 19 coincides with Route B at this point and reference to the new crossing is made under that heading.

At the south end of the new bridge a section of New Jersey State Highway No. 35, reconstructed in 1940, supplies an improved alignment through South Amboy to Morgan. An extension of this to Lawrence Harbor is under construction, scheduled for completion late in 1942. This involves new bridges over Cheesequake Creek and the New York & Long Branch Railroad.

Through Morris and Somerset counties sections of Route B have been widened and repaved at various dates, totaling nine miles. In Bergen County Route B corresponds to a short section of projected New Jersey State Highway No. S-4B, and a new cross-county route. Progress is reported on the former under Radial Route No. 11½. The latter has been included in the Master Plan adopted by the County Planning Board in 1940.

The complete development of Route B through Westchester County calls for a mixed traffic route paralleled by a parkway type highway. Developments along the latter for the past four years are described in the preceding Bulletin.

Rural Belt Highway (Route C).—From Amityville northerly to New York State Highway No. 109 on Long Island, this route has been improved as State Highway No. 110. This consists of widening and the installation of a new pavement of a variable width and was completed in November 1939.

Between Harriman and Central Valley, in Orange County, Route C has also been widened and rebuilt (completed in November 1938) as a part of New York State Highway No. 32.

Outer Branch of Route C (Route C-2).—Construction of a new pavement was completed in January, 1938, on the section of this route in Suffolk County, Long Island, following New York State Highway No. 112 from Patchogue to Medford.

In Putnam County a new alignment of U. S. Highway No. 6 for a distance of one mile east of Brewster has been provided and a new pavement installed in October, 1941. Plans for extending this to the Connecticut State line have been completed by the New York State Department of Public Works. The extension is planned over new right-of-way for its entire length.

---

[1] Under construction November, 1941, scheduled for completion June, 1942.
[2] Formerly Cross Island Boulevard.
[3] Part of this now called Southern Parkway.

---

[1] Merged with the Triborough Bridge Authority on February 8, 1940.
[2] Opened on July 3, 1941. Later in the year this was extended to Beach Channel Drive and 112th Street.

| | | 1928 — 1940 | | | | 1936 — 1940 | | | |
| Diagrammatic classification of routes | Total length in miles | Progress reported | | Construction or under construction | | Progress reported | | Construction or under construction | |
		Mileage	Per cent	Mileage	Per cent	Mileage	Per cent	Mileage	Per cent
Metropolitan Loop and Extensions:									
Mixed traffic facilities	117	63	54	48	41	7	6	7	6
Parallel routes for passenger cars	49	....	....	....	....	35	72	35	72
Inner	252	161	64	98	39	27	11	25	10
Radial	1,343	942	70	608	45	204	15	112	8
Outer Circumferential	513	131	26	123	24	28	5	24	5
Supplementary	356	122	35	102	29	27	8	22	6
Total	2,630	1,419	54	979	37	328	12	225	9

SUMMARY OF HIGHWAY PROGRESS ON MAJOR ROUTES
(As shown on map on reverse side)

INNER ROUTES

Within the Metropolitan Loop is a gridiron pattern of inner routes consisting of three east-west and nine north-south arteries connecting with the principal radials. This is supplemented by a number of diagonal connections classified as "S" or supplementary routes and a few parkway or boulevard routes classified as "P" routes. Development advancing both of these types of routes is reported along with the inner routes.

The present extent and character of progress along major routes in the central part of the Region is shown on the map in Figure 3. Progress along parkway types of routes has been described in the preceding Bulletin.

Progress for the past four-year period is reported on 27 miles of inner routes of which 25 miles were construction.

East-West Routes

On the three east-west inner routes, which involve crossing both the Hudson and East rivers, a total progress of 12 miles is reported for the past four years, of which eight miles have been or are being constructed. Description of these developments follows:

Lower Route (Inner Route I).—This highway extends from Livingston in Essex County to Springfield in Queens County. In New Jersey a small section, following Belleville Turnpike from Newark Turnpike to the projected New Jersey State Highway No. 10, was improved by widening and elimination of two railroad grade intersections. The improvement involves a viaduct about one-third of a mile long and was completed in 1937.

The portion of the route in Manhattan extending from the Holland Tunnel to the Manhattan Bridge, has had an interesting history. In 1922 the late Nelson P. Lewis, as director of

Courtesy, New Jersey State Highway Department

BRIDGE ACROSS PASSAIC RIVER ON OLD LINCOLN HIGHWAY

The Pulaski Skyway which appears in the background is limited to light passenger vehicles.

engineering studies for the Regional Plan, developed studies for an elevated highway in the center of Canal Street. Subsequent studies were made in 1929 for the publication of the Plan and in 1939 in connection with the Battery-Brooklyn Bridge controversy. Studies have been made by the City Planning Commission and the Borough President's office, and in November, 1940, the Triborough Bridge Authority included it in a proposed program of National defense directed toward filling in vital gaps in the New York highways.

Through Brooklyn and Queens the route follows Atlantic Avenue and Southern Parkway.[1] During 1939 construction on the removal of grade intersections with Long Island Railroad tracks along Atlantic Avenue from East New York to Dunton was started and is scheduled for completion on October 1, 1942. This improvement calls for the depression of tracks and the development of a highway above them.

A connection between Atlantic Avenue and Conduit Boulevard is being built as part of the Atlantic Avenue improvement. An extension of this along a widened and improved Conduit Boulevard will eventually form a continuous connection between Atlantic Avenue and Southern Parkway.

The eastern end of the route has been supplied with a dual central express roadway for light passenger vehicles with four-lane service roadways on each side for local and commercial traffic. This was completed in May, 1941 as part of the Belt Parkway.

Central Route (Inner Route II).—This route runs about midway through the center of the area within the Metropolitan Loop, from the eastern part of Queens County to Totowa in Passaic County. At the last report of progress, construction of its two major river crossings was under way and the small section utilizing New Jersey State Highway No. 3 was completed.

In the latter part of 1937 construction on the south tube of the Hudson River crossing (Lincoln Tunnel) including its approach on the New York side was completed and on December 21st of that year opened to carry two-way traffic.

On May 2, 1938, the shell of the second tube was "holed through" and shortly afterward the concrete work finished. Completion of the tube including its New York approach was deferred at this time because highway facilities leading to the tunnel could not accommodate traffic from two tubes. Work was

Courtesy, New Jersey State Highway Department

THOMAS ALVA EDISON MEMORIAL BRIDGE

Supplementing the Victory Bridge across the Raritan River for relief of traffic to the resort areas along the Atlantic.

---

[1] Formerly Sunrise Highway.

Courtesy, New York City Tunnel Authority

PORTAL AND PLAZA OF QUEENS MIDTOWN TUNNEL

View looking toward Manhattan, showing relation of tunnel alignment to the uptown area.

resumed on June 1, 1941, and is scheduled for completion in 1943, including the New York City approach.

Contracts for the construction of the New Jersey approach to the tunnel were awarded July, 1937, and this section of the route was formally opened June 30, 1939. It extends from the tunnel plaza to connect with New Jersey State Highways 1 and 3 at the eastern edge of the Hackensack Meadows and provides express movement for three lanes of traffic in each direction.

Before the completion of the Lincoln Tunnel the desirability and necessity of a distributor route for directional traffic to the southwest was recognized by the Regional Plan Association. Accordingly a freeway type route was laid out on the Graphic Regional Plan as a southwest tunnel approach across the Hackensack Meadows to connect with proposed State Highway No. 10 at Belleville Turnpike and thence to extend southerly across

the Passaic River to State Highway No. 25 in Newark. This proposal has since received recognition by the New Jersey State Highway officials and is included in their plan of metropolitan New Jersey highways as a needed facility.

From State Highway No. 3 in East Rutherford the route follows projected State Highways S-3 and 6 to the Metropolitan Loop near Totowa. Construction of roadways, including a viaduct across Berry's Creek and the Erie Railroad, is at present under way from the previously graded section of this route across the Meadows to its intersection with Rutherford Avenue and State Highway No. 2. Completion of this portion is scheduled for the latter part of 1942.

Proceedings are at present under way for widening Rutherford Avenue which will extend this proposal over the Passaic River to Passaic Avenue in Clifton. From this point, an entirely new right-of-way 180 feet in width is being graded to its junction with State Highway No. 6 at Valley Road.

The Queens Midtown Tunnel, the East River crossing on this route, previously reported as under construction, was formally opened to traffic on November 15, 1940. At the dedication ceremony the chairman of the New York City Tunnel Authority publicly expressed his appreciation to the Regional Plan Association for the invaluable aid early studies of the project by the Association had played in arrangements determining the financing of its construction.

A new six-lane elevated express highway from the tunnel plaza at Hunters Point to the cloverleaf intersection at Borden and Meeker avenues was also completed and opened with the tunnel. This extends the route approximately 1½ miles over the length previously reported and is the chief improvement in Queens to accommodate anticipated tunnel traffic. Ultimate plans for this approach road extend this portion of Route II along Borden Avenue to the intersection of World's Fair[1] and Queens boulevards. It is included on the City Planning Commission's Master Plan of Highways and will be constructed at some later date.

Upper Route.—This extends from Bayside on Long Island across the Harlem section of Manhattan to Paterson, New Jersey. In New Jersey a section following New Jersey State Highway No. 6 from State Highway No. 2 at Hasbrouck Heights to its intersection with the New York, Susquehanna & Western Railroad in East Paterson was completed in December, 1937. From this point a new proposed cut-off to the Market Street Bridge extends the route through Paterson over existing thoroughfares.

The above section is part of an improvement which has been completed to Clifton and includes a new bridge over the Passaic River. This latter part is diagonal in direction and corresponds to Supplementary Route S-8. From Clifton the supplementary route extends to Valley Road near Great Notch. This was graded during 1940 and construction was awaiting appropriation of funds.

This route includes a future vehicular tunnel under the Hudson River and crosses Harlem in the vicinity of 125th Street, entering Queens via the Triborough Bridge.

In its course along Northern Boulevard the section from Lawrence Street to Kings Road in Flushing was reconstructed as a six-lane dual highway during 1938. The improvement extends over Lawrence Street and includes a new bascule type bridge over the Flushing River. The improvement removes an old bottleneck along the route and will materially aid traffic between the Triborough Bridge and north shore communities.

Diagonal Route S-24 in Northern Queens extends Astoria Boulevard in a southeasterly direction to the Metropolitan Loop (Francis Lewis Boulevard) in the Bellaire section of Queens where Radial Route 2 extends it eastward as a new arterial through the central part of Long Island. A large part of this proposal follows the old Stewart Railroad right-of-way and

---

[1] Formerly Horace Harding Boulevard.

Courtesy, Typographical Bureau, Borough of Queens

WOODHAVEN BOULEVARD BEFORE AND AFTER IMPROVEMENT ·
View at left shows grade intersection with the Long Island Railroad taken in April, 1927.
View at right was taken in May, 1941, from a point south of the viewpoint of the other picture;
railroad grade separation can be seen in background.

has the endorsement of the New York City Planning Commission.

An important artery supplementing east-west facilities in Queens is World's Fair Boulevard (P-33). This was extended from Rodman Street westerly across Flushing Meadow Park to Queens Boulevard. Completed in September, 1937, it provides relief both to Northern Boulevard and to Grand Central Parkway.

Northern Boulevard (S-24) was widened and repaved between Woodside and Flushing following the removal of trolley tracks in 1938.

North-South Routes

Of the nine inner routes running approximately from north to south progress has occurred on six—Routes "a," "b," "e" and "f" in New York, and Routes "d" and "g" in New Jersey.

On Route "g" below the Passaic River the alignment has been moved from State Highway No. 25 easterly to a position along the Central Railroad of New Jersey to coincide part of the way with legislated State Highway No. 100 which has been studied by the State Highway Department.

Route "d" coincides with legislated State Highway No. 100 between State Highway No. 6 in Bergen County and a point opposite Tonnelle Avenue traffic circle, having received official study between these points.

Progress on Route "a" in Manhattan includes the extension of the West Side Elevated Highway from Canal to Duane streets and the completion of Henry Hudson Parkway.

On Route "b," most of which will be limited to light passenger vehicles, progress included a ramp connection between the tunnel approach to the George Washington Bridge and the Harlem River Driveway (opened to traffic in June, 1940); submission of a plan for the Harlem River Drive southerly to the Triborough Bridge to the Board of Estimate by the Borough President and completion of several sections of the East River Drive; starting construction on the Battery-Brooklyn Tunnel in October, 1940, which will connect both Routes "a" and "b" with Route "e" in Brooklyn.

Progress on Route "e" consisted of Meeker Avenue widening; new high-level bridge over Newtown Creek; and construction of an express highway along Laurel Hill Boulevard. Further advancement of the route has been the selection of a new alignment south of the Queens Midtown Tunnel, bypassing the down-

town section of Brooklyn. Hicks Street, to be widened as an outlet of Gowanus Parkway (partly completed in November, 1941) is included in the new alignment. Fourth Avenue parallels Gowanus Parkway as an approach to the proposed Narrows Crossing. Completion of Major Deegan Boulevard as a modern express artery improved Route "e" for a mile of its length in The Bronx.

On Route "f" progress has occurred on the part of Connecting Highway utilized by this route, namely, the section along the New York Connecting Railroad between Queens and Astoria boulevards. Progress consists of official adoption and a start on construction. The southerly part of Route "f" has been shifted to follow the railroad to a point opposite Fresh Creek Basin.

On the inner Supplementary Route S-29, consisting of Woodhaven and Cross Bay boulevards, construction of the section between Queens Boulevard and Forest Park was completed in midsummer of 1937 and the project for widening the route south of the park to Rockaway Boulevard in Ozone Park was opened to the public in December, 1940. Cross Bay Boulevard trestle and bridge have been rebuilt from Big Egg Marsh to the Rockaway Peninsula and extended across the peninsula to the beach front improvement. This section of the route was sponsored by the New York City Parkway Authority as a self-liquidating project and was opened as a ten-cent toll crossing on June 3, 1939. Widening of the last unimproved section of this route across Big Egg Marsh was completed in May, 1941.

RADIAL ROUTES

The radial highway system of the Regional Plan is comprised of 21 major general traffic routes which are supplemented by ten parkway routes. These routes radiate from the Metropolitan Loop to the edges of the Region where 16 of them connect to trunk line arteries leading to other centers. At the Loop the system of inner routes, described above, extends the radials through the central area of the Region.

The extent of progress for the twelve-year period is illustrated in Figure 2. The figures in circles are the route designations of the Regional Plan highway system. A description of progress on individual routes during the past four years follows:

Courtesy, New York City Tunnel Authority

BATTERY-BROOKLYN TUNNEL

The Brooklyn portal with the ventilation building above.
Construction started on the tunnel in October, 1940.

Route 1—Sunrise and Montauk Highways on Long Island.—
During the past four years the section of this route which follows the Southern Parkway[1] in Queens County has been completely rebuilt as part of the Belt Parkway. This is a one-mile
stretch extending from Springfield Boulevard (Metropolitan
Loop) to Laurelton Parkway at Rosedale. Other physical improvement of this route was limited to a grade crossing elimination on the Sunrise Highway at Lynbrook.

Preliminary studies for improvement of the route between
Patchogue and Center Moriches have been completed by the
New York State Department of Public Works. It is designed
as a dual highway, two lanes in each direction, and involves
a new alignment between Mastic and Center Moriches.

Route 2—Through Central Long Island.—A small section of
this from New York State Highway No. 109 easterly through
Farmingdale was widened to a width varying between 36 and
53 feet. Construction was completed in July, 1939.

Route 3—Jericho Turnpike on Long Island.—In September,
1938, a four-mile bypass along this route north of Riverhead
was completed. The improvement extends over new right-of-
way from Calverton to Aquebogue and consists of a four-lane
dual roadway.

Plans have been completed by the New York State Department of Public Works to widen the section of this route from
the junction of State Highway No. 25A easterly to Old Country
Road (Riverhead Bypass). Two lanes to be added along the
south side will be separated by a mall from the existing roadway.

*Route 4—Northern Boulevard, North Hempstead Turnpike,
and North Country Road.*—A high-level viaduct to carry this
route across the head of Hempstead Harbor at Roslyn as shown
on the Graphic Regional Plan was approved by the War Department, but construction was delayed by lack of funds.[2]

In 1937 the reconstruction of the antiquated railroad underpass
on North Hempstead Turnpike east of the proposed Roslyn viaduct was completed.

Route 5—General Traffic Highway to Boston.—This route
serves mixed traffic along the north shore of Long Island Sound.
A spur (Route 5-A) connects the Whitestone Bridge to the
main route at the point south of the Bronx-Pelham Parkway.

In Westchester County it follows the projected Pelham-Port

[1] Formerly Sunrise Highway.

[2] Under the program adopted by the voters of the state on November 4,
1941 this will be financed by funds diverted from railroad grade crossing
elimination bonds.

Chester Freeway, the right-of-way for which has been acquired
by the Westchester County Park Commission.

In New York City the southern end of the route (5-A) was
opened to traffic on October 11, 1941, by the Triborough Bridge
Authority and provides a direct connection to the Hutchinson
River Parkway from the Whitestone Bridge. The Association
contended that its location was ultimately the proper site for
a freeway to take mixed traffic from the future Pelham-Port
Chester Parkway as well as the light passenger traffic from
Hutchinson River Parkway.

In conjunction with supplying adequate outlets for the Triborough and Whitestone bridges, Eastern Boulevard is being
widened and repaved by the City from the Bronx River to
Pelham Bay Park. The permanent efficiency of this is doubtful
unless immediate measures are taken to protect and insure free
flow of traffic. Ultimately a new extension through Pelham Bay
Park along the New York, New Haven & Hartford Railroad
to connect with the Pelham-Port Chester Freeway will be
required.

Route 7—Radial Route through Central Westchester.—In
1938 a section utilizing New York State Highway No. 22 was
realigned and widened along the east side of Kensico Reservoir
from Valhalla to New York State Highway No. 120. The
improvement provides for four lanes of traffic and includes a
new bridge across an arm of the reservoir.

Another section on a new right-of-way between Katonah and
Goldens Bridge was under construction in October, 1941. The
program of the State Department of Public Works lists the
extension of this improvement to the Putnam County line to be
completed within three years, including a grade separation structure at Croton Falls.

Route 9—Along the West Shore of the Hudson River.—A
new alignment has been selected for this route below Hook
Mountain, consisting of New York State Highway No. 303 in
Rockland County and following a new right-of-way two miles
further west to New Jersey State Highway No. 4. The latter
was studied and adopted by the Bergen County Planning Board.

Construction on the Storm King Bypass along U. S. Route
9-W has been completed with the last and final link opened in
August, 1941. The improvement consists of a four-lane dual
roadway and extends from the Bear Mountain Bridge northward
to a point on U. S. Route 9-W about 2½ miles south of Newburgh.

Route 11—Northwest Radial of Expressway System.—This
route extends New Jersey State Highway No. 2 (Radial Route
10½) from U. S. Route 202 in Bergen County to the limits of
the Region at Chester and, with the exception of a proposed new
bypass of Harriman, follows New York State Highway No. 17.

In Rockland County a portion of this route between the State
line and Ramapo was widened from 30 to 44 feet during 1937.
Early the following year another section from the Orange
County line to Southfields, where a new cut-off is proposed to
Monroe, was widened from a three-lane to a four-lane highway.
Just east of the limits of the Region at Chester, a grade cross-
ing elimination of the Lackawanna & Hudson railroad tracks
was completed in 1937.

The future program of the New York State Department of
Public Works calls for a traffic separation north of Hillburn
at the junction of Routes Nos. 17 and 59 and also for the
relocation of Route No. 17 to by-pass Sloatsburg.

Route 11½—Arcola to Greenwood Lake.—Starting at the
Metropolitan Loop at Radburn just east of Paterson this route
follows projected New Jersey State Highway S-4B to its terminus on Outer Circumferential Route C at the south end of
Greenwood Lake.

As early as 1932 the right-of-way for this new route was
determined between Radburn and U. S. Route No. 202 in Oakland. In 1937 the portion from Oakland over the Ramapo
Mountains to a point on the existing road leading to Greenwood
Lake at the northern part of Wanaque Reservoir was surveyed.

Courtesy, New Jersey State Highway Department

NEW JERSEY STATE HIGHWAY NO. 6 AT PINE BROOK, MORRIS COUNTY

Later in that year a section of this from Oakland to the Passaic County line was graded. During 1939 the route was graded between Fairlawn Avenue in Radburn and Lafayette Avenue in Hawthorne.

In the early stages of development of this route, officials of communities through which it passes were conscious of the ill effects such an artery can have if not properly treated. To safeguard local interests they are cooperating in a joint effort to prevent this from becoming a "motor slumway." Existing zoning and planning powers of the communities are being employed to develop a type of highway which will insure a permanent, efficient route for through traffic with the least detrimental effect on abutting property.

Briefly, their plan prohibits any future conversion of residential zoning along the route to commercial use and also contemplates the refusal to approve new subdivisions which do not provide a park strip to serve as a separator between the central through traffic roadway and service roads. Several new developments along the route have already complied with this program.

Route 13—To Lake Hopatcong and Scranton via Delaware Water Gap.—This route extends from Inner Route II at Totowa in Passaic County and follows New Jersey State Highway No. 6 to Rockaway where a new connection is proposed to State Highway No. 10 to bypass some of the communities in Morris County. It follows the latter to Ledgewood where it again picks up and follows State Highway No. 6 to the limits of the Region.

The portion of this route between the Whippany River and Denville in Morris County was subject to several major improvements during the past four years. These consisted of widening, realigning, division of existing traffic lanes into divided roadways and construction of new dual roadways. Slightly over nine miles of the route were modernized with the final section completed during the middle of 1940. The grade intersection of the route with State Highway No. 5N at Denville is scheduled for elimination by the summer of 1942. The future program of the State Highway Department includes modernizing the portions of this route from Singac to Bloomfield Avenue and from Netcong to Lake Hopatcong Road.

Route 15—From Kenilworth to Phillipsburg and Harrisburg.—A section of this route in Union County from Scotch Plains to Mountainside following New Jersey State Highway No. 29 has been reconstructed with a dual roadway. This improvement was accomplished by widening and separating the lanes by the use of concrete "channelization blocks."

Route 16—From Mountainside in Union County to Philadelphia via Lambertville.—This route coincides with Radial Route 15 for a short distance in Westfield and Scotch Plains and branches off the latter to continue along New Jersey State Highway No. 29 to the edge of the Region to join New Jersey State Highway No. 30 at Flemington.

The portion westward from its junction with Radial Route 15 to Somerville has been made into a dual highway by widening and separating opposing traffic lanes with a mall constructed of "channelization blocks."

Route 17—Express Highway to Trenton and Philadelphia.—This was originally laid out to provide an express highway from the southwest to the center of the Region. In its course it utilized New Jersey State Highways Nos. 25, S-26, and 26. In the last report of progress, the premature obsolescence that had taken place and the measures to "modernize" this route were pointed out.

Since that time the New Jersey State Highway Department released plans of a new parallel route between Woodbridge and Elizabeth with northerly outlets connecting back into State Highway No. 25 and State Highway No. 1 in Bayonne via a new high-level bridge over Newark Bay.

Studies by the Association for the comprehensive handling of traffic in this section of New Jersey concluded that a parkway should be provided for shore traffic and additional facilities for general traffic. The Graphic Plan has been revised so that Radial Route 17 follows the State's alignment to Elizabeth whence it extends north to connect with the diagonal approach to the Lincoln Tunnel and Legislated Route 100. North of Bay Way Avenue (Metropolitan Loop) this becomes Inner Route "g" and south of this point at Rahway a proposed connection extends the State's proposal to follow State Highway No. 25. The section between Rahway and Woodbridge has been retained in the regional highway system as Supplementary Route S-2. The section of State Highway No. 25 between Rahway and the Metropolitan Loop has also been retained as Supplementary Route S-2½.

During the past four years additional sections of Radial Route 17 south of Rahway have been widened and traffic malls installed. The future program of the State Highway Department includes the elimination of grade crossings at all important intersections along this stretch of the route.

Route 19—South Amboy to Freehold and Lakewood.—This route extends from its starting point on the Metropolitan Loop in Staten Island, via the Outerbridge Crossing and existing state highway routes in New Jersey, through Middlesex and Monmouth counties to the southern limits of the Region.

The part which follows Hylan Boulevard in Staten Island has been widened to four lanes in each direction throughout its length from Rosebank to Great Kills. From this point a short connection is proposed to extend the route to and along Amboy Road for a distance of about 2½ miles. This portion has been widened and curves eliminated. Both of these sections were completed during 1939.

In New Jersey a section of the bypass from a point near Woodbridge to Smith Street, Perth Amboy, which was completed in 1939, supplies an improved approach to carry the route over the new Raritan River Bridge. This is a high-level structure and was officially dedicated on November 15, 1940, as the Thomas Alva Edison Memorial Bridge. It is a fixed-span type with a vertical clearance of 135 feet.

A short section through South Amboy to connect with State Highway No. 35 was completed during 1937. South of the traffic circle in South Amboy the route was widened and reconstructed in 1939 as far as Cheesequake. From there south a new alignment of New Jersey State Highway No. 4 was completed during 1940 over new right-of-way to Gordon's Corners just south of Freehold where the proposal joins old State Highway No. 4 and follows it to the southern limits of the Region.

Supplementary Radial Routes.—Progress has occurred on

Courtesy, Pennsylvania Turnpike Commission

PENNSYLVANIA TURNPIKE
An expressway extending from a point near Harrisburg to the environs of Pittsburgh,
the outstanding freeway in America.

three supplementary radial routes, one in Orange County and two in Middlesex.

On Route S-1, consisting of New Jersey State Highway No. 25 below New Brunswick, a four-mile cut-off was under construction in 1941, bypassing Deans and Dayton.

Route S-2, connecting New Jersey State Highway No. 25 with the Thomas Alva Edison Bridge and bypassing Woodbridge and Perth Amboy, was completed in 1940.

Route S-15 in Orange County, part of New York State Highway No. 17, was improved with an additional lane between Southfields and Harriman, completed in 1937.

Supplementary Parkway Radials

Supplementing the general traffic radials discussed above, the regional highway system includes ten radial parkways which would, in general, be available only for passenger vehicles. Progress on these has been described in the preceding Bulletin and will not be repeated here, but they are listed below with a few additional details as to their importance and extent:

1-B—Southern State Parkway, Long Island.

2-B—Central Parkway on Long Island.—This comprises Grand Central Parkway, Northern State Parkway and an extension of the latter eastward to and including the Montauk State Parkway.

5-B—Merritt Parkway from Putnam Lake in Greenwich to Stratford.—This is extended across Connecticut beyond the Region by the Wilbur Cross Parkway.

6-B—Hutchinson River Parkway and Extension.—This runs from Pelham Bay Park, New York City, includes all the Hutchinson River Parkway and that part of the Merritt Park-

way west of Putnam Lake in Greenwich and would eventually extend northward from that point to meet Radial Route 6.

7-B—Bronx River Parkway.—This includes all the Bronx River Parkway, its extension northward to Hawthorne Circle in Westchester County and its projected southerly extension across The Bronx.

8-B—Saw Mill River and Eastern State Parkways.—This includes, in addition, the Bronx River Parkway Extension north of Hawthorne Circle and a connection with Route 7-B via Mosholu Parkway in The Bronx. It extends northward beyond the borders of the Region.

9-B—Palisades Parkway.—This includes the extension of this projected parkway from the north end of the Palisades to Bear Mountain Park now being studied by the Palisades Interstate Park Commission through funds made available by the 1941 New York State Legislature.

10-B—Saddle River Parkway.—A possible alternative for this is a route along the Pascack River included in the Master Plan adopted in 1940 by the Bergen County Planning Board.

13-B—Lake Hopatcong Parkway.—This would follow or parallel sections of the abandoned Morris Canal west of Little Falls.

New Jersey Shore Parkway.—Largely part of Circumferential Route B-1, this would provide a radial parkway from Rahway to the shore resorts in Monmouth and Ocean counties.

EXPRESSWAYS

An expressway is simply a motor vehicle roadway designed to carry relatively large volumes of through traffic with speed and safety. In case the right of access from abutting property is denied, such a route, if open to mixed traffic, is a freeway and when open only to light passenger vehicles it is a parkway. Various fea-

MERRITT PARKWAY

An expressway in Connecticut constructed as a parkway and limited to light passenger vehicles.

tures of expressway design when applied to highways to which the abutting owners have the traditional right of access, may make an expressway temporarily or partially—such features as grade separations, central dividing strips, service roads, super elevations on curves, vertical and horizontal curves of large radii and broad shoulders—but it cannot be emphasized too much that a large part of the money spent on such improvements is wasted in metropolitan areas where there is no limitation on the access to the roadways.

The concept of the express routes needed for the Region has changed since the publication of the Plan[1] by expansion to include the principal through routes in the Region. The emergence of freeway legislation and the success of parkways in New York and Connecticut make such a network as shown in Figure 4 appear within the realm of practicability. In fact many of the lesser routes not indicated in the illustration should be freeways or parkways if and when they are established over new rights-of-way.

In the expressway system proposed for the Region there are 1,240 miles. Of these, 732 miles are for mixed traffic and 508 miles for passenger cars only. About one-fourth of the total mileage is in existence as express routes, nearly 85 per cent of which are parkways. New York State accounts for 84 per cent of today's parkway

mileage, Connecticut 16 per cent, and New Jersey none.

Freeway Legislation

Several states have enacted legislation permitting the construction of freeways or limited access highways. New York and Rhode Island passed freeway laws in 1937, followed later by Connecticut, California, West Virginia, Colorado, Maryland, Michigan and Ohio.

The routes shown as proposed are those deemed most necessary and practical to develop as expressways either by the inclusion and improvement of existing roadways or parallel alignments. A comparison of this map with that of Figure 2 will reveal the existing routes to which the expressways are related.

PROGRAM FOR DEFENSE AND POST-WAR ACTION

With a background of an analysis of progress that has taken place in a broad way throughout the past twelve years and one in more detail for the past four, a program is offered herewith for the advancement of mixed traffic highways within the next four years. These have been correlated with the requirements of recreational traffic described in the preceding Bulletin. A map illustrating the location of projects included in the program is shown in Figure 5 on page 14. Immediately below the map recommended action on each project is listed.

Practically all of the projects contained in the pro-

---

[1] Compare REGIONAL PLAN, VOLUME I. Page 268, and Information Bulletin No. 33, "The Freeway, a Modern Highway for General Traffic in Metropolitan Area," December 14, 1936.

gram are in the intensively developed sections of the Region where traffic has increased faster than adequate facilities could be provided. The program is designed to supply those missing links in the proposed regional highway system which will do most to correct prevailing congestion, particularly where it is more acute by reason of the emergency. Most of the program is aimed at post-war construction although several proposals are advanced as vital links in the defense highway system. The order of presentation does not imply an order of urgency but follows a clockwise numbering system used to locate the projects on the map.

Action on 1937 Program

Sixteen proposals for the development of general traffic facilities of the regional highway system were included in the 1937 program of public works. Nine were recommended for construction and seven for official adoption or further study. Construction has taken place in whole or in part on seven of these proposals including two projects which were advanced further than the Association recommended. Five of the projects have been adopted as parts of the master plans of New York City and Bergen County. Following is a tabular summary of the progress on each of the projects in this earlier program :[1]

Project	*Action to Date*
Midtown Manhattan Underpass	Adopted on Master Plan.
Relief of New York State Highway No. 17	Existing roadway widened. No action taken on parallel relief road.
Southwest Approach to Lincoln Tunnel	Preliminary study by New Jersey State Highway Department.
Pelham-Port Chester Freeway	No action.
Creedmoor Freeway	Adopted on Master Plan.
Long Island Approach to Queens Midtown Tunnel	Completed to Meeker Avenue. East of this point it has been adopted on the Master Plan.
Brooklyn-Queens Express Highway	Partly completed; another section officially authorized. Remainder adopted on the Master Plan.
Metropolitan Loop Highway	In Queens, its final link is under construction. The Bronx section and Narrows Crossing have been adopted on the Master Plan. No action on New Jersey section.
New Jersey State Highway No. S-3	Under construction.

[1] For parkways included in this program see previous Bulletin.

Project (continued)	*Action to Date*
New Jersey State Highway No. 21	No action.
Atlantic Avenue	Scheduled for completion October 1, 1942.
Crosstown Express Highway in Vicinity of Canal St., Manhattan	Adopted on Master Plan.
Park Avenue Improvements, Manhattan	Adopted on Master Plan.
Northerly Express Highway Approaches to Triborough and Whitestone bridges	Partly realized by completion of the Hutchinson River Parkway Extension.
Hamilton Avenue-Battery Tunnel	Under construction.
Express Highway on East Side of Hackensack Meadows	In Bergen County, adopted on Master Plan. No action taken in Hudson County.

Construction

Considered in the light of financial resources and availability of materials, all of the projects listed for construction cannot be completed within the next four years. They are presented under this classification as the more urgently needed major highways in the regional system and represent projects which should be constructed as rapidly as practical considerations will permit. Certain of the projects, due to their relation to National defense should be given preference.

A description of projects classified for construction is given below, the numbers referring to the map and list on page 14. Parts of Projects Nos. 18 and 21 are listed only for adoption and acquisition of right-of-way.

1. *Springfield-Rahway Freeway*

This extends from New Jersey State Highway No. S-24 at Springfield southerly across Union County to Rahway where it would connect with the proposed Shore Parkway and State Highways Nos. 4 and 35. Construction should be synchronized with that of the proposed Pleasant Valley and Shore parkways.

3. *Diagonal, Newark Airport to Lincoln Tunnel*

Since this project was presented by the Association in the 1937 program, the section across the Hackensack Meadows has been included in the New Jersey State Highway Department's program but with no definite commitment as to its construction. The completion of the north tube of the Lincoln Tunnel will make it urgent that this be built at an early date.

5. *New Jersey State Highway No. 21*

This section extends north from the recently completed section at Clay Street, Newark, to connect with the proposed Passaic River Parkway. As an important link in a proposed continuous route along the Passaic River from Newark to Paterson it should be built in the immediate future.

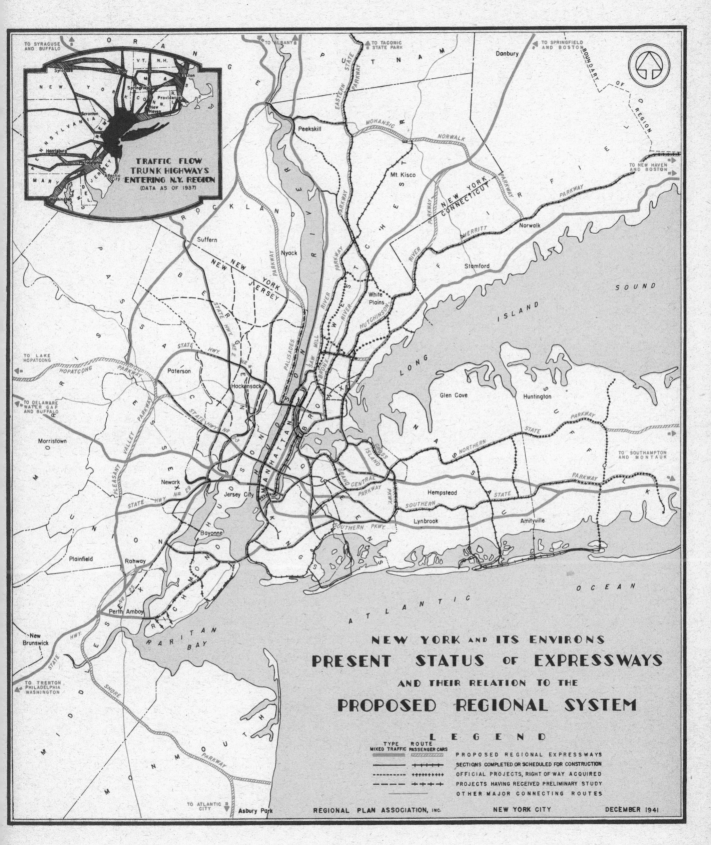

TRAFFIC FLOW
TRUNK HIGHWAYS
ENTERING N.Y. REGION
(DATA AS OF 1937)

NEW YORK AND ITS ENVIRONS
PRESENT STATUS OF EXPRESSWAYS
AND THEIR RELATION TO THE
PROPOSED REGIONAL SYSTEM

LEGEND

TYPE	ROUTE	
MIXED TRAFFIC	PASSENGER CARS	PROPOSED REGIONAL EXPRESSWAYS
		SECTIONS COMPLETED OR SCHEDULED FOR CONSTRUCTION
		OFFICIAL PROJECTS, RIGHT OF WAY ACQUIRED
		PROJECTS HAVING RECEIVED PRELIMINARY STUDY
		OTHER MAJOR CONNECTING ROUTES

REGIONAL PLAN ASSOCIATION, INC.   NEW YORK CITY   DECEMBER 1941

FIGURE 4

7. *New Jersey State Highway No. S-3*

This project, extending from the east side of the Passaic River at Rutherford to New Jersey State Highway No. 6 at Great Notch, is part of a direct approach to the Lincoln Tunnel from the Paterson area. A start has been made on preliminary construction consisting principally of rough grading.

8. *New Jersey State Highway No. S-4B*

This provides for a new highway approach to the Greenwood Lake area extending from New Jersey State Highway No. 4 in Arcola. It also forms an additional northwest outlet, paralleling State Highway No. 2. The right-of-way has already

River Parkway Extension in order to relieve the Post Road and provide a strategic highway between the Port of New York and the important defense industries along the Connecticut shore. If the section of Hutchinson River Parkway Extension, opened this fall, were made available weekdays to mixed traffic, an express route for commercial vehicles would be provided to both the Whitestone and Triborough bridges, the latter via Eastern Boulevard and Whitlock Avenue (see Project No. 13).

13. *Northeast Approach to Triborough Bridge*

This proposal contemplates the provision of facilities along Whitlock Avenue and Eastern Boulevard from the Triborough Bridge to Hutchinson River Parkway Extension which will

Courtesy, New Jersey State Highway Department

JOHN DAVISON ROCKEFELLER MEMORIAL HIGHWAY

Sections of existing state highways from the vicinity of Camden to Belmar in Monmouth County were designated by the New Jersey Legislature in 1938 as parts of this route. The above view was taken along the developed section in Burlington County outside of the Region, where a right-of-way of 520 feet has been provided. The highway is opened to mixed traffic and a 40-foot strip on each side of the right-of-way has been reserved for future marginal roads.

been acquired and several sections graded. It should be completed within the next four years.

11. *Pelham-Port Chester Freeway and Its Extension in New York City*

As early as 1925 the Westchester County Park Commission sought to relieve the Boston Post Road by a new route from the state line at Port Chester to Pelham at the New York City line. The Association proposes that this be extended south along the railroad through Pelham Bay Park to the Hutchinson

permit uninterrupted movement of traffic. Completion of this and the Pelham-Port Chester freeway in the immediate future is essential for expediating the movement of mixed traffic to and from New England.

15. *Midtown Manhattan Underpass*

This is essential to provide an express route between the east and west sides of the port and to alleviate local street congestion in midtown Manhattan. The financial success of both the Lincoln and Queens Midtown tunnels are in part dependent on this project.

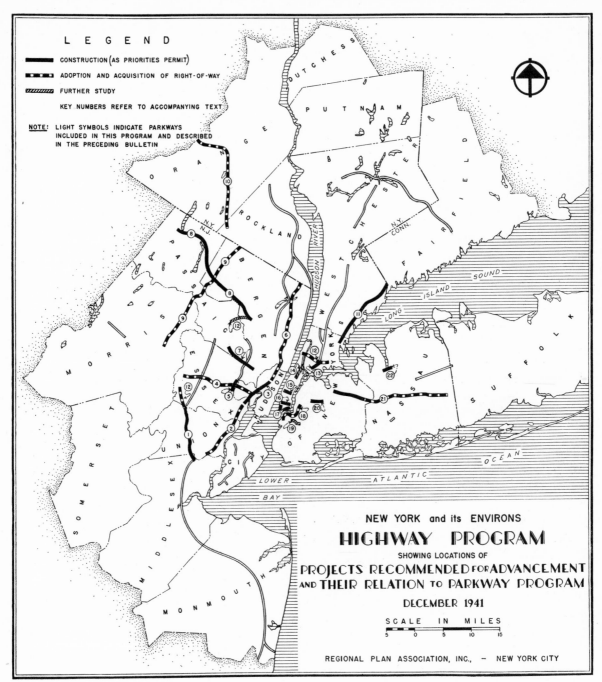

FIGURE 5

Recommended Action: A—Construction (as priorities permit); B—Adoption and acquisition of right-of-way; C—Further study.
NOTE: For parkways included in this program see preceding Bulletin.

Key No.	Project	Action	Key No.	Project	Action	Key No.	Project	Action
1.	Springfield-Rahway Freeway	A	9.	Metropolitan Bypass in New Jersey	B	17.	Southerly Extension of West Side Elevated Highway and East River Drive	A
2.	Relief Route to New Jersey State Highway No. 25, Rahway to Newark Airport	B	10.	Relief of New York State Highway No. 17	B	18.	Brooklyn-Queens Crosstown Express Highway	B
3.	Diagonal, Newark Airport to Lincoln Tunnel	A	11.	Pelham-Port Chester Freeway and Its Extension in New York City.	A	19.	Express Connection between Atlantic Avenue and Manhattan Bridge, Brooklyn	C
4.	New Jersey State Highway No. 10.	B	12.	Metropolitan Highway Loop......	B & C	20.	Easterly extension of Queens Midtown Tunnel Approach..........	A
5.	New Jersey State Highway No. 21.	A	13.	Northeast Approach to Triborough Bridge	A	21.	Creedmoor Freeway	A & B
6.	North-South Freeway in Bergen & Hudson counties	B	14.	Park Avenue Improvement, Manhattan	C	22.	Roslyn Viaduct, Nassau County....	A
7.	New Jersey State Highway No. S-3.	A	15.	Midtown Manhattan Underpass ...	A			
8.	New Jersey State Highway No. S-4B	A	16.	Crosstown Express Highway in Vicinity of Canal Street, Manhattan	A			

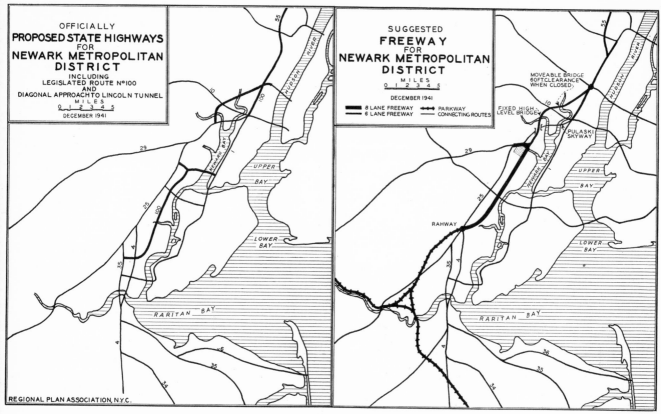

FIGURE 6

A STUDY (RIGHT) FOR IMPROVED NEW JERSEY APPROACHES TO INTERSTATE HIGHWAY CROSSINGS,
COMPARED WITH THE PROPOSALS (LEFT) OF THE STATE HIGHWAY DEPARTMENT

16. *Crosstown Express Highway in Vicinity of Canal Street, Manhattan*

This consists of an elevated structure connecting the Holland Tunnel and West Side Highway with the Manhattan and Williamsburg bridges. A plan for such a connection was released by the Association in the controversy over the Battery-Brooklyn crossing. Studies have been made by several public agencies since that time and the project has grown in public esteem. What is now needed is the adoption of a definite plan so that actual construction may proceed as soon as possible.

17. *Southerly Extensions of West Side Elevated Highway and East River Drive*

The extensions of these arteries are important to obtain the full benefits of the new Battery-Brooklyn Tunnel. Construction of these should be scheduled with that of the Tunnel.

20. *Easterly Extension of Queens Midtown Tunnel Approach*

An extension of the Queens Midtown Tunnel approach from the Meeker Avenue Bridge traffic circle, along Borden, Caldwell, and Eliot avenues to connect with World's Fair Boulevard at Queens Boulevard should be constructed within the next four years. In the more distant future an express highway south of this to connect with Interboro Parkway and give access to the Jamaica Bay area and south shore of Long Island, will have to be provided.

21. *Creedmoor Freeway*

As indicated in the 1937 program this project calls for a limited access highway from the intersection of Astoria and Northern boulevards at Flushing along the old Stewart Railroad right-of-way and into Nassau County utilizing the old Motor Parkway for most of its way to the Babylon-Farmingdale Road. This would provide for mixed traffic a much needed express highway connecting the central part of the Region with the central and south shore of Long Island. Within the immediate future, construction should be started on the Queens section and a definite plan adopted including the acquisition of missing links for its extension in Nassau County.

22. *Roslyn Viaduct, Nassau County*

This project is included in the immediate construction program of the New York State Department of Public Works. Its completion will eliminate a serious bottleneck along Radial Route 4 of the regional highway system.

Adoption and Right-of-Way Acquisition

Experiences of the last depression clearly showed that the lack of plans seriously delayed action toward relieving unemployment. As an approach to problems after the peak of defense expenditure the Association recommends that definite plans be prepared and that the rights-of-way be acquired in the immediate future so that a "work reservoir" will be created to lessen the severity of any future employment crisis. The following projects are recommended for adoption and acquisition of right-of-way. Parts of the project listed as No. 12 are suggested for further study.

2. *Relief Route to New Jersey State Highway No. 25, Rahway to Newark Airport*

This would replace New Jersey State Highway No. 25 between Rahway and Newark Airport with a permanent type of express route. From Rahway to Elizabeth it follows Legislated Route 100. Plans for a northerly extension of this to Newark Airport should be adopted and the right-of-way of the entire project acquired.

4. *New Jersey State Highway No. 10*

The status of this project, envisioning a freeway extending easterly from Livingston across Essex County to the Belleville Turnpike in Hudson County, has not changed since it was listed for adoption and mapping in the previous program of urgent projects. It is still urgent that a definite plan should be adopted and its right-of-way acquired.

6. *North-South Freeway in Bergen and Hudson Counties*

This constitutes parts of Inner Route "d" and Radial Route 9, extending from the Lincoln Tunnel approach northerly through Hudson and Bergen counties. Following the easterly edge of the Hackensack Meadows it extends across Overpeck Creek to continue along the west side of the Overpeck Meadows; thence it continues north through several Bergen County communities to connect with New York State Highway No. 303.

A program for the immediate future should include the adoption of a definite plan and a start in the acquisition of its right-of-way. The communities in Bergen County through which this project passes can materially aid in determining its alignment by intelligent control of new subdivisions and cooperation with the County Planning Board.

9. *Metropolitan Bypass in New Jersey*

This involves a route parallel to U. S. Highway No. 202 along the west shore of the Ramapo River from the New Jersey State line near Suffern to Pompton Lakes and a southerly extension of this over new right-of-way to New Jersey State Highway No. 6 near Parsippany. The project is designed to replace a part of U. S. Highway No. 202 with a modern roadway along a more direct alignment for traffic destined for New England from points south. It is also a strategic link in the coastal defense highway system. A plan for its alignment should be adopted and a start made on acquisition of its right-of-way.

10. *Relief to New York State Highway No. 17*

The need is still apparent for the section of this proposal between Hillburn and Southfields as listed for adoption and acquisition in the previous program of the Association.

North of Southfields, adoption and acquisition of a new align-

ment to the limits of the Region at Chester is included in this program. The New York State Department of Public Works' future program includes a similar proposal to Middletown.

12. *Metropolitan Highway Loop*

The present status of the Loop can be seen on the map in Figure 1. Sections of the Loop which should be advanced in the immediate future are:

(a) A direct route to cross The Bronx from the Whitestone Bridge to George Washington Bridge tunnel approach including a new bridge over the Harlem River. Adoption and acquisition of the entire section should be started within the next four years.

(b) Study should be given to an adequate location of the Metropolitan Loop north and west of Paterson where it would connect State Highway No. S-4B at Radburn and State Highway No. 6 at Totowa.

(c) The section through the gap in the Watchung Mountains between Summit and Millburn presents special difficulties. A plan for this should be worked out by the New Jersey State Highway Department in cooperation with local authorities and a definite right-of-way determined and acquired.

18. *Brooklyn-Queens Crosstown Express Highway*

Segments of this route north of Meeker Avenue Bridge are completed, under construction, or officially mapped. The section between the projected Battery-Brooklyn Tunnel approach at Hamilton Avenue and the southerly plaza of Meeker Avenue Bridge still requires study. A definite plan should be adopted for this section and the right-of-way acquired within the immediate future.

Further Study

The following two projects by reason of their complicated physical design and cost require more detailed study than the Association could give. It is hoped that officials responsible for providing these facilities will give due consideration to their advancement.

14. *Park Avenue Improvement, Manhattan*

On the assumption that the improvement of Park Avenue north of 96th Street with a direct connection across the Harlem River to Grand Boulevard and Concourse in The Bronx will ultimately be required, a plan developed by the Association showing its location was presented in the 1937 program. A final plan should be worked out jointly by the city and the New York Central Railroad.

19. *Express Connection between Atlantic Avenue and Manhattan Bridge, Brooklyn*

An express connection between Atlantic Avenue and the Manhattan Bridge Plaza is needed as an adequate channel for traffic to and from the bridge. A preliminary study by the Association envisions bypassing the busy intersections of downtown Brooklyn. It should receive further detailed study by city officials.

AIR TRANSPORTATION HAS REDUCED THE BARRIERS OF TIME AND SPACE

IV. TRANSPORTATION AND PUBLIC SERVICES

The Port of New York requires a series of terminals —rail, water and air—and the progress on the development of these and the approaches serving them during the past five years, 1937-1941, and the relation of these to the proposals incorporated in the Graphic Regional Plan are summarized in the first part of this Chapter. The latter part is devoted to a similar review of new developments in public health services and in public housing.[1]

With the exception of "defense" housing and some terminal improvements essential to the war effort, little immediate progress is likely to be made in these types of construction. After the war there must be a renewed effort in these fields to catch up with current needs and to provide for a shift to a more normal program of employment. Now, therefore, is an appropriate time to review what exists today and to point out some of the most urgent needs.

Expansion of the railroad system in the Region is still largely in the planning stage. The outstanding physical developments are the completion of the West Side Railroad Improvement in Manhattan and striking advances in the elimination of railroad-highway grade crossings in both New York and New Jersey. The airport system is being steadily improved to meet greatly increased demands for air transport and the development of new landing fields has been accentuated by the war.

In the field of other public services steady progress has been made on the purification of the waters of the harbor through the construction of sewage treatment plants, notably in New York City but also in New Jersey. Public housing, a new development within the

period under review, has made remarkable progress, but at the present time is limited to such projects as are essential for housing industrial workers in those districts where war industries have greatly increased the concentration of population.

RAIL TRANSPORTATION

New trends in freight and passenger transportation are chiefly responsible for lack of development of new rail facilities proposed in the Regional Plan. The Plan aims at a program to integrate all media of transportation into a coordinated system eliminating duplication of service and its accompanying waste.

Conditions caused by new modes of transport call for the establishment of new methods to handle the mounting flow of traffic. The Association and other interested agencies have given study to the problem and prepared plans to meet changed conditions.

In addition, recent activity has taken place on three specific railroad proposals incorporated in the Regional Plan, on an unprecedented number of railroad grade crossing eliminations throughout the Region and on city rapid transit lines which have been extended and brought into a unified system.

Terminals for New Modes of Transportation

Modern highways have opened new lines of communication in competition with the railroads, particularly those terminating in New Jersey. Much of the Jersey railroad freight is still ferried from rail terminals to piers throughout the harbor and many passengers still use ferries to cross the Hudson River to Manhattan. Motor trucks, buses and subways distribute other loads to convenient destinations. Street congestion resulting from the increasing use of buses and trucks is approaching a point where the convenience

---

[1] For similar reviews for earlier years, see FROM PLAN TO REALITY (1933), pp. 84-93, 97-101, and FROM PLAN TO REALITY, TWO (1938), Chapters IV and VIII, published by the Regional Plan Association, Inc.

of this mode of transportation is being rapidly offset by numerous delays.

During 1939 the Port of New York Authority began to formulate a program for establishing union terminals for truck freight, and negotiations with motor truck operators were under way by the end of the year. On February 5, 1942, plans for a $2,000,000 terminal (see Figure 1) were completed and the Port of New York Authority urged its construction as a war-time emergency measure to expedite truck shipments and to relieve street congestion by elimination of part-load trucking. At a hearing held February 24, 1942, this project was endorsed in principle by trucking, civic and business interests, who urged its immediate construction.

Construction and operation of a union bus terminal at 42nd Street and Ninth Avenue were approved on January 15, 1941, by the City Planning Commission. The plans of a $4,000,000 structure were approved by the Board of Estimate on January 23rd of that year. These included a tunnel to connect the terminal with the Manhattan approach to the Lincoln Tunnel. The Association had made studies of this problem in 1939 and recommended a terminal at a site one block further east, with an off-street approach above ground instead of in a tunnel.

Trunk Railroad Lines

Advancement of the trunk line railroad features of the Regional Plan has occurred on the following two proposals:

Greenville-Bay Ridge Freight Tunnel.—This is the keystone of the Comprehensive Railroad Plan for the Port of New York (Connecting Line No. 12) which would link the important railroads on the west side of the harbor with Brooklyn, thence via the New York Connecting Railroad with The Bronx and railroads of New England. The importance of the proposal has been recognized for a long time but its failure to advance beyond the plan stage has been principally due to the difficulty of getting an agreement with the railroad companies for its use which would permit self-liquidating financing.

A report by the Port of New York Authority filed with the New York State Legislature during 1938 showed that a one-track tunnel with a capacity of 5,000 freight cars daily could be built for $57,000,000. To make the tunnel self-supporting the operation of 1,400,000 cars annually would be necessary. Under conditions existing at that time inadequate traffic made the project economically impractical. The most recent prospect for action is the effort by the Port of New York Authority to

Courtesy, New York Central System

REBUILT 30TH STREET RAILROAD YARDS OF NEW YORK
CENTRAL RAILROAD

A part of the completed West Side Improvement.

finance the project as a national defense measure with non-interest bearing federal funds to be repaid from future earnings.

West Side Freight Line, Borough of Manhattan.—The depressed section of the relocation of the New York Central Railroad tracks (Connecting Line No. 18) on the west side of Manhattan between 30th Street and 60th Street yards and the covering of the tracks through Riverside Park were completed during 1937. Construction of a spur to the stockyards at West 41st Street was completed during 1938, and the reconstruction of the 30th Street Yards in 1941. These are part of the West Side Improvement and their completion has done much to rehabilitate the west side of Manhattan, to facilitate movement of railroad freight and to release street surface for vehicular movement. The entire project included removal of 105 grade crossings.

Railroad Grade Crossing Eliminations

Elimination of many dangerous railroad grade crossings throughout the Region is necessary for public safety and also for the expeditious movement of vehicular traffic. The ground work for a program to achieve this end in the New York sector of the Region was provided by the state constitutional amendment of 1925 and its subsequent revision of 1927. Having failed to accomplish its objective, the amendment was again revised in 1938 and approved in the general election of that year. This segregated $50,000,000 from a total of $170,000,000 for New York City use and also removed certain obstacles which had hindered the elimination of grade crossings in both the city and rest of the state.

Elimination of railroad grade crossings in New Jersey has been considerably advanced with the aid of Federal funds. Under jurisdiction of the Board of Public Utility Commissioners, construction of the various projects has been undertaken by the State Highway Department.

New York City.—Through the Transit Commission, the State of New York, in the latter part of 1939, started work on an extensive program of railroad grade intersection removals within the City of New York. In Staten Island the Great Kills-Huguenot, Richmond Valley, and Tottenville grade elimination projects were completed during 1940. The balance of the program for this part of the city, calling for complete grade eliminations between Grant City and New Dorp, Oakland Heights and Bay Terrace, is under construction, but completion of the latter section has been deferred until after the war.

In Brooklyn and Queens the Atlantic Avenue project extending from East New York to Dunton involves the elimination of 20 grade intersections of the Long Island Railroad. This project is about five miles long and places the railroad tracks underground with a modern highway above. It is to be completed as rapidly as delivery of materials permits.

On June 20, 1940, construction of railroad overpasses at Linden Boulevard and the Belt Parkway in the Aqueduct section of Queens were completed. Contracts for the elimination of all grade crossings along the Old Southern Branch of the Long Island Railroad from Jamaica to the city line at Rosedale have been cancelled due to shortages of materials.

On the Rockaway peninsula a project involving elimination of 39 crossings of the Long Island Railroad on the 5.5-mile section from the City line at Far Rockaway to Rockaway Park has been completed. The two-track railroad has been elevated on a viaduct designed for either Long Island Railroad or City Subway

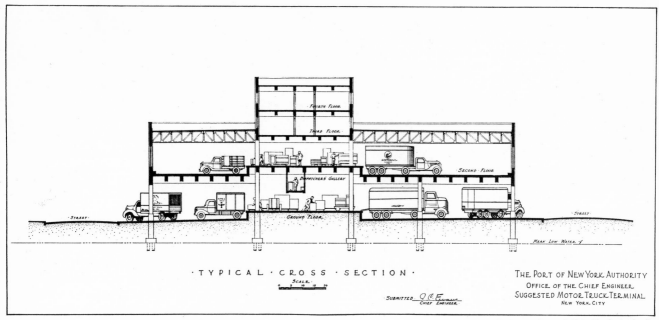

· T Y P I C A L · C R O S S · S E C T I O N ·

SCALE.

SUBMITTED _____
CHIEF ENGINEER.

THE PORT OF NEW YORK AUTHORITY
OFFICE OF THE CHIEF ENGINEER
SUGGESTED MOTOR TRUCK TERMINAL
NEW YORK CITY

Courtesy, Port of New York Authority

FIGURE 1

rolling stock. About 1.7 miles from Hammels to Rockaway Park were placed in operation during the early part of 1941.

Other less important projects for New York City in the Transit Commission program include grade separations at Long Island City, Maspeth, VanDine Avenue, 105th Street and Little Neck Road. Construction of these is planned as part of a post-war program. Their completion will make New York City 100 per cent free of railroad grade crossings.

In the Environs.—In New York counties of the Region outside of New York City the Public Service Commission through the Department of Public Works has completed a total of 23 railroad grade eliminations during the past four years. The Commission has ordered elimination of 57 additional grade crossings which are distributed as indicated in the accompanying table. Construction on these projects will proceed as priorities of materials permit.

GRADE CROSSING ELIMINATION PROJECTS IN THE
ENVIRONS OF NEW YORK

County	Completed 1937-1941	Under construction	Future program
NEW YORK STATE			
Nassau	7	4	34
Orange (part of) . . .	6	....	....
Rockland	1	....	2
Suffolk	5	....	8
Westchester	4	3	13
Total New York State	23	7	57
NEW JERSEY			
Bergen	5	....	1
Essex	2	....	....
Hudson	2	....	....
Middlesex	12	1	6
Monmouth (part of) . .	1	....	....
Morris	3	1	....
Passaic	1	1	1
Union	17	....	2
Total New Jersey . .	43	3	10
CONNECTICUT			
Fairfield (part of) . . .	2	....	....
Total for Environs . .	68	10	67

In New Jersey counties of the Region a total of 43 railroad grade crossings have been eliminated since the report of progress four years ago and three additional projects are under construction. The largest project involved removal of 14 street intersections of the Central Railroad of New Jersey within the City of Elizabeth. Elimination of ten more grade crossings has been ordered by the Board of Public Utility Commissioners. As in the case of proposed projects in New York State, completion of these hinge on their relation to National defense.

Railroad grade crossing eliminations in the Connecticut section of the Region have been limited to construction of two projects in the Town of Wilton. There are no projects under way or contemplated for future construction.

Suburban Rapid Transit

For the past decade, daily rail commutation between New Jersey and New York has failed to hold its own against the convenience of passenger car and bus transportation. To counteract this trend an interesting innovation, combining rail service of the New York, Susquehanna & Western Railroad from Paterson to the Susquehanna transfer at North Bergen with bus connections to Manhattan via the Lincoln Tunnel, went into operation during 1939. Modern streamlined Diesel powered trains and a trainside bus transfer enables a time saving which reduces the trip to 30 minutes whereas formerly 60 minutes were spent to reach Times Square.

The Association holds that neither bus nor private passenger car is the solution for peak-hour mass transportation of people. A coordinated system of suburban rapid transit, along with a better urban distribution to serve the suburban areas of New Jersey, Long Island and Westchester County, is still needed. Such a system was incorporated in the Regional Plan and

TYPICAL ELIMINATION OF RAILROAD GRADE CROSSINGS

View at left shows section of Long Island Railroad tracks looking east from Beach 108th Street, Rockaway Park, New York City.
View at right shows Erie Railroad tracks crossing over Mill Street, Belleville, New Jersey.

developments toward its realization reported in previous reports of progress. More recent activity on rapid transit in New Jersey is as follows:

Pursuant to direction of the State Legislature in 1938, continued and extended study was given to the problem of northern New Jersey rapid transit by the Port of New York Authority. Surveys of railroad and ferry passenger traffic have been completed and conclusions drawn. Definite physical and financial plans have been formulated, including means of effectuating an initial step of the proposed system. In addition, drafts of legislation to permit operation and maintenance by or under the Port Authority were prepared.

Pending conferences with a special legislative committee to advise on legislative policy, complete financial plans have been withheld.

City Rapid Transit

Maximum efficiency in mass movement of passengers within the City of New York is assured by the recent unification of all the city's subway lines. Ownership of the I.R.T. and B.-M.T. subway and elevated lines was taken over during 1940 enabling the city to coordinate operation of all rapid transit lines within its borders.

Operation of the Ninth Avenue and Second Avenue elevated lines above 60th Street was discontinued and the structures demolished. The two-mile Sixth Avenue line of the Independent System was placed in service December 15, 1940, and the Fulton Street line, now under construction, is scheduled for operation in 1943.

Demolition and removal of the Broadway elevated structure spur from Havemeyer Street to Kent Avenue and a similar fate of the Fulton Street line between Brooklyn Bridge and Rockaway Avenue were the first physical steps to rid Brooklyn of outmoded transit facilities.

Demolition and removal of the elevated structure in Park Row from Brooklyn Bridge to Chatham Square was authorized on April 20, 1941, by the State Legislature.

On May 15, 1941, the four and one half mile Dyre Avenue-180th Street section of the old New York, Westchester & Boston Railroad in The Bronx was placed in operation as part of the City's rapid transit system. In the studies of the Regional Plan, the Westchester & Boston line was a part of a proposed regional suburban rapid transit system. After operation of the railroad was terminated in 1937, the Association was active with other groups to keep the right-of-way for rail use rather than have it abandoned or used for other purposes.

PORT DEVELOPMENTS

Although world wide shipping schedules have been realigned since the outbreak of hostilities, New York Harbor is playing an important role in our national policy of "Arsenal of Democracy."

During May, 1940, New York City's newest pier, Number 64, located at the foot of West 24th Street, was taken over by the Panama Line to assist in carrying out the "Lend-Lease" policy. Enlargement of the Brooklyn Navy Yard, the development of new naval repair facilities and supply depot in Upper Bay and conversion of the country's first "free port" at Stapleton, Staten Island,[1] into an army supply depot are some of the principal results on the harbor of our military effort.

Other activities during the past four years pertaining to marine transport and facilities conceived for a more efficient transfer and distribution of water-borne cargoes are discussed below.

Channel Improvements

Shifting sands, river silt and the accumulation of harbor wastes require perennial attention to maintain adequate channel depths. Deepening and maintaining navigable waterways throughout the United States is largely carried out by the Federal Government with direct responsibility of the work under the United States Army Engineer Corps.

During the past four years, dredging operations have been continued along main ship channels of New York Harbor. These include deepening the 2,000-foot Hudson River Channel to 45 feet south from 54th Street to the harbor entrance, and Buttermilk and Red Hook channels between Brooklyn and Governors Island to 35 and 40 feet, respectively. Projects have been under way on other less important waterways, including Kill Van Kull, Arthur Kill, Newtown Creek, Harlem River Ship Canal, Coney Island Creek, and Bronx River.

Funds for improvements on minor channels have been proposed by the Rivers and Harbors Committee of Congress in

---

[1] This activity has been temporarily transferred to five piers on the west side of Manhattan.

1941. Projects in New York State include Jamaica Bay, Jones Inlet, Lake Montauk, and Northport, Peconic and Larchmont harbors. Shark River and the Intercoastal Waterway have been selected in New Jersey for improvement along with annual maintenance of the Passaic River. Work is to proceed at such time as will not materially interfere with national defense.

Naval Drydock and Supply Base

In keeping with a national policy of providing repair facilities at strategic locations in ports throughout the country, the United States Navy Department, after considering the merits of available locations in the New York Harbor, selected a site for such use in Upper Bay offshore of Bayonne.

Advantages for large-scale port development in this area of the New York Harbor were pointed out on the Graphic Plan. The soundness of the Association's attitude in opposing a Battery-Brooklyn Bridge on the grounds that adequate defense of the harbor required that no obstructive crossing be built seaward of naval repair bases is recognized in the selection of this location.

In the last report of progress, plans for the development of a large rail-marine terminal at this location were described. The project was completed in January, 1939, and was operated for commercial shipping until March, 1941, when the Federal District Court in Newark ordered Bayonne City officials to turn the terminal over to the Navy Department for the sum of $2,837,000.

Since that time the original area has been enlarged, contracts have been signed and work started on the construction of a graving dock which is designed to accommodate the largest naval vessels afloat or projected. In addition to docking and repair facilities, development of the remainder of the site as a naval supply depot has also been started.

Wholesale Food Markets

A general picture of the movement of food supplies to the Port of New York and its subsequent distribution to points throughout the Region was presented in the Regional Survey.[1] Within the past few years there has been active study given by local, state and federal agencies to the improvement and relocation of the wholesale food markets in New York City, all of which are of regional importance. A summary of these developments is given below.

Primary Produce Terminal.—In 1938 the New York City Department of Markets proposed a public, union produce terminal on Manhattan to replace the privately-owned Washington market and to expedite the transfer and distribution of produce. At the request of the Mayor, the United States Secretary of Agriculture appointed a committee to investigate, in cooperation with state and local agencies, the problem and its solution. A Special Report[2] on this subject was published by the United States Department of Agriculture in 1940, which recommended that "a new, complete, modern wholesale fruit and vegetable market be constructed." After reviewing available sites, the conclusion was reached that "the new market be built at the western end of Long Island on some site between the

Williamsburg Bridge and the Queensboro Bridge.... Other uses should be found for the present Washington Street market area and the produce piers, so that dealers can dispose of their property in this location on some equitable basis and move into the new market."

In June, 1940, after ascertaining the reaction of the trade to the Department of Agriculture Plan, the Mayor requested the Port of New York Authority to develop a plan for utilizing the city-owned waterfront in lower Manhattan. Such a plan, now known as the Hedden-Morgan Plan, was developed in cooperation with representatives from the Department of Markets, Department of Docks, Borough President of Manhattan, and trade advisers and submitted October 15, 1940.[1] It covered six blocks along the Hudson River waterfront between Jay and Laight streets, utilizing Piers 22 to 29 inclusive. The proposed new improvements were confined to the piers and West Street, leaving the existing market facilities along Washington and adjacent streets to take care of retail sales.

The New York State Department of Agriculture and Markets has continued its studies of the New York City market problem and has stressed the regional and national aspects of any new produce terminal. It has urged the selection of a site on Long Island accessible to water, rail, trucking, and rapid transit routes, but free of the congestion which exists in Southern Manhattan. The creation of a Market Authority, which would coordinate city, state, regional, and Federal interests was proposed to finance, construct and operate such a terminal.

Both plans were estimated to be self-supporting. Savings on the produce handling costs under both the Federal and state plans were estimated at $8,500,000. The estimated savings on the Hedden-Morgan Plan, originally set by its proponents at $6,000,000, were later increased to $9,000,000 on a basis of additional information.

It now appears that the war will postpone any immediate construction of a produce terminal and give time to select the best plan as a post-war project.

Brooklyn Secondary Market.—The expansion of the Brooklyn Navy Yard required the removal in 1941 of the farmers produce market on Wallabout Canal. A substitute site was selected in Canarsie near Jamaica Bay. It was necessary to establish temporary quarters there, and the first group of permanent structures was scheduled for completion in July, 1942.

Poultry Terminal.—In 1940 the Board of Estimate of New York City adopted a plan for a wholesale, live poultry terminal on Newtown Creek at the edge of Long Island City. This would concentrate at one point live-poultry activities, now carried on at several different sites. The construction of the terminal was started in 1941 and is now completed.

THE REGIONAL AIRPORT SYSTEM

An achievement of historic character in the exploits of aviation was marked with the arrival of the Dixie Clipper at LaGuardia Field on February 9, 1941, after pioneering a new route from Lisbon which linked four continents and set an all-high, non-stop distance record for commercial aviation.

More important, from a planning viewpoint, than daring attempts to join the ends of the earth in a "web of air" is the rapid expansion of air traffic and its obvious future growth. Not only has the total number of air passengers in the Nation surged ahead from 8,661 in 1927[2] to some 4,500,000 in 1941, but the volume of mail

[1] Regional Survey, Volume III, PHYSICAL CONDITIONS AND PUBLIC SERVICES, pages 125-133.
[2] THE WHOLESALE FRUIT AND VEGETABLE MARKETS OF NEW YORK CITY. U. S. Department of Agriculture, April, 1940.

[1] "New York City Union Freight and Vegetable Terminal," the Port of New York Authority, Development and Operations Department.
[2] Earliest date statistics are available.

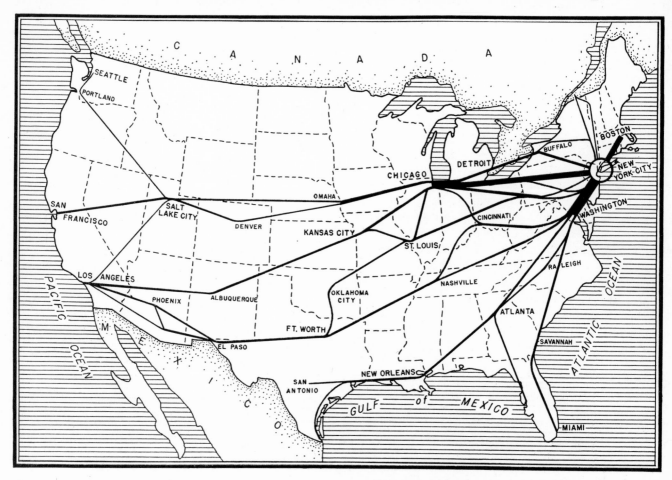

Redrawn from 1940 Annual Report of Port of New York Authority

FIGURE 2

DIRECTIONAL FLOW OF 335 REGULARLY SCHEDULED FLIGHTS CONNECTING THE PORT OF NEW YORK WITH THE ENTIRE UNITED STATES
The relative frequency of service is proportionate to the thickness of lines.

and freight carried by plane has correspondingly increased. More than 22,700 tons of mail were flown throughout the nation during 1941 contrasted with 533 tons in 1927, while air express has grown from 23 tons in 1927 to 11,250 tons in 1941.

Directional flow of commercial air traffic entering the New York metropolis in relation to that of other principal cities in the United States is pictured on the map in Figure 2. As in the case of all other transcontinental and transatlantic lines of communication, the Port of New York is the principal focal point of the world's air transportation.

Evolution of Regional System

The Association's studies of air transportation as it affects the Region have centered principally on the location of airport sites and their proper correlation with other means of communication and types of land use. When the Graphic Plan was published in 1929 the nucleus for a regional airport system had already

been established. Additional sites were proposed at that time to form a comprehensive system. Progress toward realization of the proposed system has been reported as of 1932 and 1936.

During 1940 the staff of the Association classified the regional system according to standards set up by the Civil Aeronautic Administration as a guide to future airport requirements. Briefly, the proposed system calls for four major transport terminals spaced closely around the central commercial area of the Region and a series of 17 secondary ports located in suburban areas or near satellite centers to serve training or lesser commercial needs. In addition, 25 ports are distributed throughout the Region to serve local flying interests and also supply emergency landings. The latter classification includes military ports which prohibit commercial or private flying. The proposed system is the result of a series of consultations with official agencies and representatives of the major air transportation companies.

Transport Terminals

Developments during the past four years on the transport terminals in the airport system are as follows:

LaGuardia Field.—Exceeded only by Washington National Airport, this is the largest project of its kind in the world and serves as a terminal for domestic and transoceanic planes. It provides facilities for both land and sea planes. Opened on December 1, 1939, it supplies a thoroughly integrated service for all phases of air transport. With constantly mounting schedules and ever increasing patronage, present facilities have about

program to improve landing and take-off facilities was undertaken. New drainage facilities have been installed, runways lengthened and permanent pavement installed.

Floyd Bennett Field.—This was purchased by the Federal Government and commissioned as a naval air station June 2, 1941. Along with this action all private flying is prohibited. Its return to civil use after the war is not expected.

Proposed Idlewild Airport.—To supply the ultimate needs of commercial air transport in the metropolitan area a site in the southeast corner of Queens is proposed to be developed as a major terminal to replace Floyd Bennett Field. Under the defense program the site is being developed for immediate military use. The New York City Planning Commission has made studies

Courtesy, American Airlines, Inc.

ADMINISTRATION BUILDING, LA GUARDIA FIELD
Landings and take-offs are supervised with timetable precision from the control tower
where directions are radio-phoned to pilots.

reached their capacity. The field's average of 283 scheduled flights a day is rated the biggest in the country.

Present plans of the City of New York contemplate adding 335 acres to the present site of 500 acres. Over five miles of new parallel runways will be installed; existing runways lengthened and five new hangars constructed. Completion of this expansion is planned to accommodate over double the present volume of traffic.

Newark Airport.—Previous to the opening of LaGuardia Field this was for more than ten years the principal commercial air center in the New York Region. Operations were curtailed June 1, 1940, when the four major air lines moved their terminals to New York's municipal airport. A year later (June 1, 1941) full services were resumed with a total of 52 passenger flights on weekdays and 42 on Sundays. The Civil Aeronautics Authority designated this as a co-terminal with LaGuardia Field. On April 22, 1942, it was announced that the city had leased most of Newark Airport to the War Department but that commercial airlines would continue to use the field.

Principal developments of the port include a new administration building and six new hangars. At the time of reopening, a

of the location and has made recommendations regarding highway approaches to Manhattan.

Secondary Airports

Laid out to meet the needs of civil aviation with an intended stand-by military value, six secondary sites of the proposed regional airport system, because of their strategic locations, have been selected by Federal authorities as part of the national defense program. Three of these are existing fields in New Jersey and three involve new fields in New York State. Funds for the development of the new sites and improvement of existing fields have been provided by Congress and construction of several of these are under way at present, with development of the remainder scheduled for the immediate future.

Under this program local agencies provide the land and buildings while Federal funds supply field improvements, runways, navigation aids, and other facilities. All of these sites are designed to meet standards set up by the Civil Aeronautics Authority and construction work is handled by the Army Engineers Corps.

Despite the fact that increasing military demands earmark these for immediate military services, they are ultimately intended for civil use. Their development carries out a substantial number of the proposed secondary airports of the regional system and represents a permanent contribution to aviation in general which will have a constantly increasing worth when normal conditions return. Because of the military value of detailed information concerning development of these projected airports, description of their facilities and location has been omitted, as in the case of all other airports in the Region.

Recent developments on other secondary airports[1] of the regional system consisted principally of extension and paving of runways or enlargement of the fields. Improved facilities have been provided at:

Caldwell-Wright Airport, Caldwell, N. J.
Bendix Airport, Bendix, N. J.
Christy Airport, New City, N. Y.
Bridgeport Airport, Stratford, Conn.
Roosevelt Field, Mineola, L. I.
East Hampton Airport, Wainscott Station, L. I.
Islip Airport, Islip, L. I.

Local Airports[1]

Of the 45 airports and seaplane landings of local importance distributed throughout the Region, only 25 land ports and five marine landings are called for in the regional airport system including three proposed new sites. Many of the existing facilities are poorly located with regard to their function in the coordinated airport system and are of various sizes, shapes and conditions of ownership. Most of the operators have been reluctant to construct permanent improvements and changes in number and location are frequent. Under these conditions it is difficult to justify their present or future utility.

A serious problem confronting outlying localities in the Region is that of ownership, operation and maintenance of airports. The Association believes that permanency is a fundamental essential to a well organized system and a policy of ownership, whether private or public should assure that end. The Association will cooperate with local committees which are responsible for shaping policies so as to coordinate the needs of

Courtesy, American Airlines, Inc.

TYPICAL SCENE OF AIR-FREIGHT LOADING
At the New York metropolitan air terminals annual express tonnage has grown to more than 2,700 tons in 1940, as contrasted with 47 tons in 1930.

the locality with the development of the Region as a whole.

Excluding military and naval airfields, nine airports and three seaplane bases of the regional system serving local interests have been additionally improved during the past four years. These are as follows:

Westfield Airport, Rahway, N. J.
Somerset Hills Airport, Basking Ridge, N. J.
Stewart Field, Newburgh, N. Y.
Reynolds Central Westchester Airport, Pleasantville, N. Y.
Lime Ridge Airport, Beekman, N. Y.
Westchester Airport, Armonk, N. Y.
Wall Street Skyport, Manhattan, N. Y.
Midtown Skyport, Manhattan, N. Y.
Edco Seaplane Anchorage, Queens, N. Y.
Flushing Airport, Queens, N. Y.
Grumman Airport, Farmingdale, L. I.

PUBLIC HEALTH SERVICES

Unusual activity marks the past four years progress in development of public services related to the protection and advancement of public health. Reflecting the impetus of Federal aid, the two major regional problems of water supply and sanitation have been attacked with greater results than in any similar period

---

[1] Civilian use of these has been curtailed as a war measure. As of March 5, 1942, there were 23 designated airplane and seaplane landings in the Region open to other than air-carrier or Government aircraft.

heretofore. The scope of this report does not permit recording the many community disposal plants and water works which have been completed in the period.

With the flow of Federal funds to non-defense projects stopped and with the national psychology shifted from domestic pursuits to total war production there has already resulted a marked ebb in the construction of these facilities. It will take several years for completion of projects now under way and it is hoped that Federal control of materials will be such as to permit completion of these essential services.

Water Supply

For many years the metropolitan areas of Northern New Jersey and New York, together containing over three fourths of the total population of the Region, have been almost constantly confronted with the problem of water supply. The rapidity of growth has caused existing sources to be inadequate in quantity or unsuitable in quality.

The regional aspect of the problem is demonstrated by the fact that adequate sources are to be found only at considerable distance outside of the areas concerned. Conservation of existing supplies and coordination of plans to develop new supplies are the chief concerns of planning in the interest of efficient use and just distribution of water resources.

Developments of major water supply facilities since the report of progress four years ago are as follows:

New York City.—Limitations of existing water supplies have long been recognized by the city. Fortunately, intervening years have cleared legal and budgetary hurdles so that in January, 1937, construction was started on a vast program to divert 540 million gallons of water daily from the tributaries of the Delaware and Hudson rivers into the city's distribution system. Principal elements of the project are three dams and reservoirs on Rondout Creek, Neversink River and East Branch, interconnecting tunnels, and an 85-mile pressure tunnel leading to Hillview Reservoir at the northern boundary of the city.

Construction of the first stage of the project includes the Neversink and Rondout reservoirs, a short connecting tunnel and the main Delaware Aqueduct. Work has progressed on the tunnel to about 75 per cent of completion. Surface and control works along the tunnel are more than half complete. The section of the tunnel leading from Kensico Reservoir to the city will be available by the middle of 1942 to carry a larger volume of existing stored waters at Kensico to meet the anticipated emergency of peak-summer consumption.

Completion of Rondout Reservoir and the aqueduct is expected by 1944, making 100 million gallons of water available daily with the possibility that some additional water may be drawn from the Neversink Reservoir. Exploratory caissons at the site of the latter have been completed and considerable earth moved preliminary to constructing the dam itself.

The second stage of the program includes construction of the reservoir on the East Branch and building a 26-mile connecting tunnel to bring water from it to Rondout Reservoir. This stage is designed to supply the city with additional water to the extent of 370 million gallons daily.

Northern New Jersey.—Early studies and negotiations for providing additional water supply to metropolitan New Jersey were pointed out in the report of progress four years ago. Late in 1937 the North Jersey District Water Supply and the State Water Policy commissions advocated the linking of existing systems operating to capacity with those having surplus storage facilities to stave off an imminent shortage. This was put forth as a temporary remedy with the urgency of a new major source of supply stressed.

During 1939, comprehensive legislation for providing a new major water supply system and for eventual unified control of existing sources of supply by a state authority was introduced in the State Legislature. Indorsed by Governor Moore, the proposal would divert from 150,000,000 to 230,000,000 gallons daily from the Delaware River through an aqueduct following the old Raritan Canal from Raven Rock across the state to Bound Brook. A reservoir would be constructed near Bound Brook and a connection established with the Wanaque system in the metropolitan area. As in the case of earlier proposals no definite action was taken on the plan.

A report by a six-member committee was sent to the New Jersey Legislature on November 10, 1941, stressing the need of a new state water supply and the conservation of existing municipal and privately-owned supplies. It suggested that the State Water Policy Commission, North Jersey District Water Supply Commission, Newark's water supply and the Passaic Valley Water Commission ultimately be brought under a single authority. The total cost of the project would be about $190,000,000, most of this being for part payment of existing supplies and $41,000,000 for a new supply.

The report recommends Governor Moore's proposal of three years ago and urges interconnection of existing supplies to safeguard all communities in time of drought. The report carries a recommendation of the WPA that $45,000,000 be spent for compensating reservoirs along the upper Delaware.

On January 7, 1942, Governor Charles Edison appointed a 12-man board known as Governor's Emergency Water Supply Commission. The commission has begun to study ways and means to prevent a water shortage in metropolitan New Jersey.

Sewage Disposal

Uncontrolled discharge of municipal wastes into the nearest water course has for a long time been one of the most vital matters confronting the Port of New York. Establishment of the Interstate Sanitation Commission in 1936 reflects the importance of regional regulation and control of the problem. Since that time, constant vigilance over the condition of metropolitan waterways has been maintained, and repeated efforts made by the Commission to bring about correction of contamination at its source. Despite efforts to clean up New York Harbor, periodic inspection by the commission discovered 21 separate sources of varying intensity polluting the waters of the harbor in 1941.

Connecticut's ratification, during 1941, of the pact formerly limited to New Jersey and New York, increased the geographical control of the commission and brought its program of pollution abatement a step closer to realization. Its control now extends from Sandy Hook up the Hudson River to above Bear Mountain Bridge, on the Atlantic shore to Fire Island Inlet, on Long Island Sound to Port Jefferson, and on the Connecticut shore to New Haven.

New York City.—Encouraging progress to free the harbor of pollution has taken place during the past four years, due principally to the efforts of the City of New York.[1] The effect of plants now in operation is becoming apparent in improved conditions in the boundary waters of the city, particularly in Shellbank Creek, Flushing Bay, Jamaica Bay, Harlem River, and East River.

Courtesy, Department of Public Works, New York City

JAMAICA SEWAGE TREATMENT WORKS
Aerial view of plant under construction.

The most significant advance toward abatement of pollution in the New York harbor has been the formulation and start of construction on a comprehensive program for the proper disposal of the city's wastes. The Department of Public Works has planned a total of 18 modern plants at strategic locations throughout the city to provide adequate sewage treatment facilities. These are distributed in the various boroughs as follows: two in Manhattan, two in The Bronx, five in Brooklyn, four in Queens, and five in Richmond.

The first plant of the comprehensive scheme to go into operation was the Coney Island works completed in 1935. Extension of this to double its capacity, from 35 to 70 million gallons daily, has been substantially completed. Additional flows, formerly entering Paerdegat Basin to the extent of 30 million gallons daily, were diverted to this plant during June, 1941, through a six-foot diameter trunk sewer constructed by the Borough of Brooklyn. The plant furnishes treatment by the chemical precipitation process together with chlorination during the summer months, and plain sedimentation during winter months.

Construction of Wards Island (197 million gallons daily), Tallmans Island (40 million gallons daily), and Bowery Bay (40 million gallons daily) works, together with their intercepting sewers, were well along at the time of the last report of progress four years ago. These were placed in operation in October, 1937, April, 1939, and November, 1939, respectively. Originally going into operation as a sedimentation plant, facili-

ties have been added to the Bowery Bay plant to extend the degree of treatment to include secondary treatmnt by the activated sludge process. The other two plants were the first in New York City to process final treatment by the actitvated sludge method.

Construction of an activated sludge plant with a capacity of 65 million gallons daily along the north shore of Jamaica Bay south of Aqueduct in Queens, to serve the southeastern section of Queens, is at present about 90 per cent completed. Useable portions of the old screening plant in operation at this location will be incorporated in the new works which are scheduled for operation in the latter part of 1942.

Settling, aeration, and sludge digestion tanks at the 60-million gallons daily capacity activated sludge plant in the 26th Ward are under construction. This replaces the old screening plant located along the north shore of Jamaica Bay east of Canarsie and will serve the East New York section of Brooklyn. Construction is being pushed, subject to priorities.

A new plant located at Harts Island, with a capacity of 1.5 million gallons daily and with two pumping stations, is substantially completed. This is of the plain sedimentation type with chlorination. Flow from nearby City Island will be pumped to the plant through a force main laid at the bottom of the channel. Institutional flow on Harts Island will also be pumped to the plant. While not large in relation to New York City's other plants, it will afford protection to the newly developed parks at Orchard Beach and Pelham Bay.

The design program of the Department of Public Works is being continued on new projects of the city-wide scheme, which include a 160-million gallons daily sedimentation plant in the Owls Head section of Brooklyn; the first stage of a 280-million gallons daily treatment works on Newtown Creek to serve portions of Brooklyn and Queens; a 160-million gallons daily activated sludge plant at Hunts Point in the Bronx; a 15-million gallons daily chemical treatment plant to serve the Rockaways; a plant to serve the upper west side of Manhattan; and also a project at Port Richmond in Staten Island.

Up to the present time the City has spent about $60,000,000 on the plants now in operation or under construction. In the work done so far, the City has been aided by Federal grants of $11,000,000. The completed program with facilities to accommodate immediate flows is estimated at a total of $178,000,000.

In the Environs.—In the last report of progress a procedure, as set forth by the Port Raritan District Commission, to relieve pollution of the Raritan River was described. This involved the provision of individual sewage treatment facilities by municipalities located in the Raritan valley. Further progress has been made in that area as well as other parts of the environs.

Stimulated by PWA grants and loans, 14 communities placed works in operation to handle a combined total of 30 million gallons daily. Individual plants vary in size from 0.6 to 10 million gallons daily and employ processes varying from plain sedimentation to complete treatment.

A survey of pollution in the Raritan River completed in December, 1941, showed that industrial wastes dumped into the river each day had jumped more than 50 per cent in the last four years. According to this survey by the New Jersey Department of Health, the average yearly flow of the Raritan just below its junction with Millstone River at Manville in Middlesex County was 700 million gallons daily while the summer daily average was 400 million gallons. This average dropped to about 37 million gallons daily last summer when it was observed that 23 million gallons of industrial and three million gallons of sanitary wastes were discharged into the river daily just about the head of tidewater at New Brunswick.

---

[1] The following summary of New York City projects is based on a paper presented by Irving V. A. Huie, Commissioner of Public Works, before the Metropolitan Section, American Society of Civil Engineers, May 21, 1941.

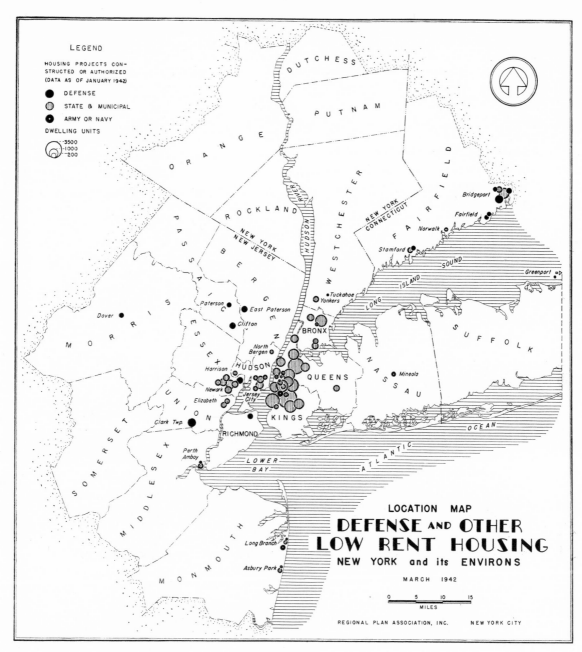

LEGEND

HOUSING PROJECTS CON-
STRUCTED OR AUTHORIZED
(DATA AS OF JANUARY 1942)

● DEFENSE
◉ STATE & MUNICIPAL
◉ ARMY OR NAVY

DWELLING UNITS

LOCATION MAP

DEFENSE AND OTHER
LOW RENT HOUSING

NEW YORK and its ENVIRONS

MARCH 1942

0   5   10   15
MILES

REGIONAL PLAN ASSOCIATION, INC.   NEW YORK CITY

FIGURE 3

As a result of the survey the New Jersey Department of Health has laid down a policy of strict enforcement of health laws and regulations to stop pollution in the Raritan River Valley. So far, municipalities and industries have spent $5,500,-000 to construct treatment plants and it is estimated that at least $1,500,000 more will be necessary for additional works to take care of industrial wastes.

In Bergen County a study of sanitary sewer requirements by the Planning Board points out that the coverage of a sewer system should be larger than the single municipality and recommends joint action preferably by groups of municipalities lying within a natural drainage basin.

Recognition of the advisability of joint treatment has since evidenced itself in the construction of several plants to serve two or more communities. Rutherford, East Rutherford and Carlstadt completed a jointly operated plant as did Hackensack and Maywood. Also, existing facilities have been enlarged at the jointly owned Dumont-Bergenfield works. A plan for a sewage treatment works along with an intercepting sewer to serve seven communities along the Overpeck Creek has been completed and at present is awaiting financial arrangements.

Pursuant to orders of the Interstate Sanitation Commission, officials of the City of Elizabeth have completed facilities for the treatment of seven million gallons of sewage which for years had discharged into the waters of Kill Van Kull. On November 30, 1941, this flow was diverted to the Joint Meeting treatment plant at Amboy Avenue, Elizabeth.

In a separate order, officials of the City of Elizabeth have been directed to undertake treatment at an early date to care for all additional sewage now being discharged by the municipality into the waters adjacent to the city.

Continued improvements and extensions to the county sewage

system in Westchester have taken place since the report of progress four years ago. Among the more important projects are the construction of trunk sewers, intercepting local Hudson River outfall sewers in the Villages of Hastings and Dobbs Ferry, also in the southern and central parts of Yonkers. A new two-mile trunk sewer extends the county system to a new residential area in the City of Rye and improvements to existing facilities in the Villages of Mamaroneck and Larchmont also have been made.

Refuse Disposal

New York City's experience with "land fill disposal" of refuse coupled with refinements in the procedure, indicates that this method is reasonably satisfactory if carefully supervised and controlled. About one third of the city's refuse (9,000,000 cubic yards) is disposed of in this fashion with a result that many acres of marshland are being reclaimed for park purposes. This method of disposing of sanitation wastes has been employed to advantage primarily at Soundview Park in The Bronx, Marine Park in Richmond and Spring Creek Park along the north shore of Jamaica Bay.

PUBLIC HOUSING

Low rent housing under public control began with limited dividend projects under the New York State Board of Housing in the twenties; then followed Federal stimulation and the establishment and operation of local housing authorities in the thirties; and finally in the emergency, the Federal government began constructing defense and war housing directly through a number of its own agencies. While there was some overlapping in point of time the three periods are fairly distinct. A picture of the total progress to date is presented in Figure 3.

Of the 73 projects in the Region occupied, under construction or approved for construction, 35 are in New York State (including 31 in New York City); 28 in New Jersey; and 10 in Connecticut. The number of dwelling units in the 73 projects is 43,019 and the total cost, $202,883,000.

Since 1937, the time interval emphasized in this report, a total of 60 projects are recorded, 28 of which are in New Jersey, 22 in New York and ten in Connecticut. Two thirds of the total number of dwelling units are in New York State, 96 per cent of these being in New York City. A summary by counties is presented in the accompanying table which gives the number of projects, number of dwelling units, total cost and unit cost. Of the 60 projects, 14 are for industrial workers, two for Army personnel and one for the Navy.

Of the 21 counties of the Region, projects have been constructed in all but five—Somerset County in New Jersey and Dutchess, Orange, Putnam and Rockland in New York State. In number of projects Fairfield County leads with ten, then New York County with eight, followed by Essex and Hudson with seven each.

The location and type of structures is of interest in the evolution of public housing as reflecting the general policies and conditions of the times. The limited dividend houses erected under the supervision of the New York State Housing Board were of the six-story apartment type constructed about a central court on part of a city block. They were different from most private buildings of the day in that they offered more light, air and open space than the great majority of contemporary struc-

PUBLIC HOUSING IN NEW YORK AND ITS ENVIRONS, 1937-1941

County	Projects	Dwelling units	Total cost	Unit cost
CONNECTICUT				
Fairfield (Part of)	10	4,141	$17,883,586	$4,537.83[1]
NEW JERSEY				
Bergen	1	400	1,906,200	4,765.50
Essex	7	2,735	14,443,792	5,277.44
Hudson	7	1,984	9,676,000	5,399.55[2]
Middlesex	2	298	1,473,000	4,942.95
Monmouth	5	659	3,180,000	4,825.49
Morris	1	300	1,344,800	4,482.66
Passaic	2	650	3,233,500	4,974.61
Somerset	0	0	0	0
Union	3	1,528	7,291,706	4,772.05
Total, New Jersey	28	8,554	$42,548,998	$5,088.37[3]
NEW YORK				
Bronx	1	400	2,310,000	5,775.00
Kings	6	10,470[4]	~~14,550,173~~	~~4,785.32~~
New York	8	8,623[8]	55,570,008[5,6]	6,144.40[7]
Queens	2	3,597	30,819,782	6,782.52[9]
Richmond	1	346	16,445,000	4,571.86
			2,282,000	6,595.37
Total, New York City	18	23,436	$107,426,790 ~~$119,666,963~~	$5,991.12[10] ~~$6,673.74[10]~~
Dutchess (Part of)	0	0	0	2 0
Nassau	1	200	845,000	4,225.00
Orange (Part of) .	0	0	0	0
Putnam	0	0	0	0
Rockland	0	0	0	0
Suffolk	1	50	not available	
Westchester . . .	2	610	3,632,000	5,954.08
Total, New York State, except New York City . . .	4	860	$ 4,477,000	$5,527.16[11]
Total, New York State	22	24,296	$111,903,790 ~~$124,143,963~~	$5,971.06[12] ~~$6,624.19[12]~~
Total, New York Region	60	36,991	$172,336,374 ~~$184,576,547~~	$5,551.35[13] ~~$5,945.64[13]~~

[1] Computed on 3,941 units.
[2] Computed on 1,792 units.
[3] Computed on 8,362 units.
[4] Construction of 1,424 of these units delayed because of war.
[5] Figures for Williamsburg Houses do not include legal fee.
[6] Figures for Fort Green Houses estimated.
[7] Figured on 9,044 units.
[8] Construction of 5,103 of these units delayed because of war.
[9] Figured on 4,544 units.
[10] Figured on 17,931 units.
[11] Figured on 810 units.
[12] Figured on 18,741 units.
[13] Figured on 31,044 units.

tures. These were mostly located in the older sections of Manhattan and Brooklyn.

Then followed larger projects with Federal assistance but still under state control of investment return: Knickerbocker Village in Manhattan, Hillside Houses in The Bronx and Boulevard Gardens in Queens. These were built in the middle thirties. The creation of a Federal housing agency brought with it the idea of slum clearance as a major objective of housing. Williamsburg Houses in Brooklyn was followed by projects in Newark, Jersey City, Bridgeport, Asbury Park and other outlying centers as well as additional projects in New York City.

War priorities have dried up all activity on housing for normal civilian use, replacing it by construction of units for war industry workers and military personnel. Homes for industrial employees have been located away from New York City where local facilities were not able to absorb the increase in population.

Housing with some degree of Federal participation is being thought of as part of a post-war program to ease the transition from wartime to peacetime industrial production. Slum clearance and the rehabilitation of blighted areas appears to be a logical objective for such a program.

V. A DECADE OF ZONING PROGRESS

Hand in hand with the physical development of the Region has gone an improvement in legislative controls over the uses of land and the types of structures that may be built thereon. Zoning, instituted in this country by the New York City Zoning Resolution of 1916, is the principal medium by which this has been accomplished.

The up-to-date population figures made available by the Federal Census of 1940 brought home to many of the older and more populous communities a realization that their zoning ordinances and maps had been based upon a future growth that will never occur, or, as is more often the case, had been made without any real analysis of the extent of business, multi-family housing and industrial requirements in the present or future. Those communities without the protection of a zoning ordinance are turning to zoning as a means of avoiding the problems of blight, which are menacing the older communities.

During the past few years interest in zoning has been particularly active in New York City where civic organizations have cooperated with the City Planning Commission in restudying certain areas and the commission has sponsored extensive revisions in the regulations. After rather acrimonious discussions on some of the new features proposed, an amended Zoning Resolution was adopted by the Board of Estimate on June 28, 1940, involving a considerable number of changes, many of them of far-reaching importance. An extensive revision of the zoning maps to bring them into reasonable harmony with the city's probable future requirements for business, industry and various types of residence is yet to follow. Its need has been felt for some years and is now recognized as urgent.

The Regional Plan Association has in its files a complete picture of the zoning in effect in the Region at the time the Association was established in 1929. This Chapter summarizes the results of an investigation of the trends of zoning development in the Region during the decade from approximately January 1, 1930, to January 1, 1940.[1] The survey involved a review of 190 ordinances in effect at the beginning of 1930 and 351 in effect at the end of the decade. There has been an increase of 84.7 per cent in the number of ordinances involving a 107.2 per cent increase in the areas under

[1] New zoning ordinances have been reported adopted during the latter part of 1940 in Cranbury Township and the City of Perth Amboy in Middlesex County and in the Borough of West Paterson in Passaic County. Since that time the Borough of Wharton in Morris County, Borough of North Haledon in Passaic County and the Town of Carmel in Westchester County have adopted zoning ordinances for the first time. In several other communities throughout the Region ordinances are under preparation or old ordinances have been comprehensively revised.
For earlier reviews see FROM PLAN TO REALITY (1933), pp. 101-106, and FROM PLAN TO REALITY, TWO (1938), pp. VII—2 and VII—7, published by Regional Plan Association, Inc.

the protection of zoning, but a large proportion of the newly zoned communities were outlying ones. The percentage of resident population enjoying the advantages of zoning has increased from 88.1 to 95.7 per cent.

While it is generally accepted that zoning is part of planning and that a zoning ordinance should, therefore, be designed to conform with a master plan for the municipality, we find that zoning has generally preceded the making of a master plan. As a result, many ordinances have, within a brief period of time, become inadequate and in need of revision. In the present survey attention has been given not only to the increase in the scope of the zoning movement, but to the improvement in the efficiency of the rules and regulations in the ordinances themselves, particularly where they would promote a better coordination between zoning and planning.

The following discussion takes up first the region-wide picture of areas zoned, then discusses the trends in both character and extent of use regulations by geographical sectors of the Region. Following this is a review of some of the outstanding trends in regulatory provisions.

INCREASE IN AREAS ZONED, 1930 to 1940

A graphic comparison of municipal areas zoned in the New York Region for 1930 and 1940 is shown in Figure 1. The number of municipalities involved is summarized by counties in the upper right-hand corner of the map, and the areas and resident population of these municipalities as compared with corresponding county-wide figures are given in the table on page 2. Referring to the map, the light hatching represents communities which had been zoned prior to 1930 and the darker shading indicates areas zoned since that time. The remaining blank areas are those municipalities in which zoning had not yet been established.

A comparison of the spread of zoning in the various counties of the Region indicates that the intensity of zoning activities is closely related to the ease of communication with New York City. Most of the area has been zoned on Long Island and in Westchester County, as well as in those New Jersey counties which have direct connections to Manhattan, such as Bergen, Hudson, Essex and Union. These counties form an inner circle within the Region in which 70 to 95 per cent of the communities, as well as of the total area, of each county are zoned. The corresponding measurement for counties in the remainder of the Region varies from 20 to 40 per cent.

In 1930, zoning was most advanced in Nassau, Westchester, Essex, and Union counties. In each of these, well over half of their communities, and a corresponding proportion of their area, had been zoned. Since that time Bergen, Hudson, Suffolk, and Fairfield counties have attained this status, with Suffolk leading in the amount of new area zoned. The greatest number of communities to have adopted zoning ordinances are found in Nassau, Bergen, and Westchester counties.

CHANGES IN CHARACTER AND EXTENT OF USE ZONES

Zoning regulations ordinarily make provision for residential, business and industrial uses. These in turn are subdivided into districts of varying intensity. While there has been a marked movement for correcting the faults of overzoning, one trend has been the creation of an increasing number of use categories, particularly for residential use. Unfortunately, these have seldom been laid out in conformity with a sound physical pattern for the community and confusion has resulted. Use districts must be designed to bear a relationship to each other, as well as to their physical environment, if zoning is to achieve its basic aim.

From a broad survey of all of the ordinances and zoning amendments adopted in the Region, upward revisions, involving a more stringent application of use zoning, can be readily pointed out. Three representative areas of the Region have been selected to give a cross section of typical use zoning practice during the past ten years. The geographical location of these areas is shown in Figure 2. Use districts, as designated in the ordinances of the municipalities or parts of same that comprise these sample areas, have been plotted in detail for the beginning and end of the period under review and an explanation of changes in each area is given. For the suburban areas, which overlap municipal boundaries, a statistical summary of the changes has also been made.

There is a big variation in the number and types of use zones adopted in the different municipalities. In order to compare these effectively, it was necessary to devise a uniform classification of uses. It was found that the ordinances for the environs could be classified under a system involving three residential classifications, one business classification and two industrial classifications. These are explained on page 8. They were not applicable to zoning in New York City.

New York City

The original Zoning Resolution in New York City established only three use zones: residential, business and unrestricted. The boundaries of these were shown on the use map and separate maps were employed showing height districts and area districts. A different set of district boundaries apply to each of these three sets of maps. The system is still in effect, although it is not

COMPARISON, BY COUNTIES, OF THE EXTENT OF MUNICIPAL AREAS ZONED IN 1930 AND 1940, WITH PERCENTAGES OF TOTAL AREA AND POPULATION RESIDING IN ZONED COMMUNITIES FOR THE TWO PERIODS, NEW YORK AND ITS ENVIRONS

County	Area of county, square miles	Zoned areas as of				Per cent of resident population in zoned areas	
		January 1, 1930		January 1, 1940		1930	1940
		Square miles	Per cent	Square miles	Per cent		
NEW YORK STATE							
New York City (5 Counties)	297.4	297.4	100.0	297.4	100.0	100.0	100.0
Dutchess (Part of)	115.7	0.0	0.0	0.0	0.0	0.0	0.0
Nassau	273.4	166.6	60.9	271.8	99.4	59.7	99.9
Orange (Part of)	415.1	79.1	19.1	212.7	51.3	5.1	23.0
Putnam	241.0	0.0	0.0	86.2	35.8	0.0	11.9
Rockland	183.0	7.7	4.2	104.5	57.1	29.7	72.5
Suffolk	915.1	128.5	14.0	569.8	62.3	25.5	81.4
Westchester	446.2	219.7	49.3	382.0	85.6	95.4	99.5
Total New York State	2,886.9	899.0	31.1	1,924.4	66.6	94.8	98.3
NEW JERSEY							
Bergen	235.8	85.4	36.2	183.7	77.5	58.8	96.4
Essex	127.4	95.4	74.9	117.0	91.8	94.1	99.9
Hudson	44.1	25.7	58.3	39.7	90.0	67.8	86.5
Middlesex	308.8	11.1	3.6	89.3	28.9	25.5	50.5
Monmouth (Part of)	426.7	19.4	4.5	45.1	10.6	37.9	56.2
Morris	477.7	31.7	6.6	125.0	26.2	44.8	61.3
Passaic	198.9	30.3	15.2	62.9	31.7	86.5	95.8
Somerset	305.1	2.9	1.0	62.2	20.3	15.0	63.9
Union	103.4	61.4	59.3	98.6	95.4	53.3	99.5
Total New Jersey	2 227.9	363.3	16.3	823.5	36.9	67.6	87.2
CONNECTICUT							
Fairfield (Part of)	413.2	207.9	50.3	297.7	72.1	88.7	95.3
Total Region	5,528.0	1,470.2	26.6	3,045.6	55.4	88.1	95.7

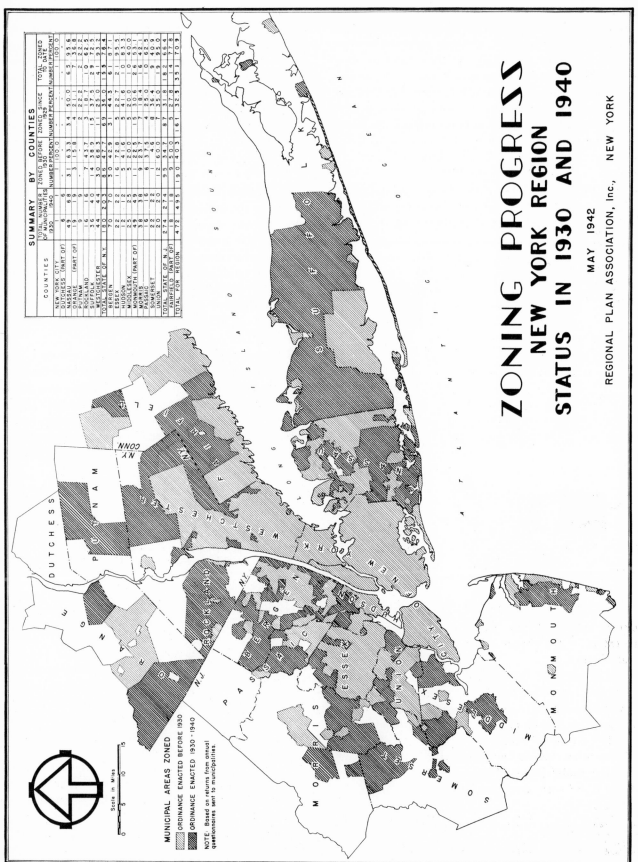

SUMMARY BY COUNTIES

COUNTIES	TOTAL NUMBER OF MUNICIPALITIES		ZONED BEFORE 1930		ZONED SINCE 1929		TOTAL ZONED TO DATE	
	1930	1940	NUMBER	PERCENT	NUMBER	PERCENT	NUMBER	PERCENT
NEW YORK CITY				100.0				100.0
DUTCHESS (PART OF)	4	6	3	63.3	3 4	50.0	6 5	95.6
NASSAU	6	68	5	65.8	3 4	22.1	6 7	95.8
ORANGE (PART OF)	19	9	2	22.2	2	22.2	2	22.2
PUTNAM	9	9	2	22.2	10		2	22.2
ROCKLAND	16	16	7	43.7	3	18.7	10	62.5
SUFFOLK	36	40	14	38.9	15	37.5	29	72.5
WESTCHESTER	44	44	30	68.3	11	25.0	41	93.2
TOTAL STATE OF N.Y.	180	203	86	47.7	69	34.0	155	86.4
BERGEN	70	70	30	42.9	31	44.3	61	87.1
ESSEX	22	22	16	72.8	5	22.7	21	95.5
HUDSON	12	12	5	41.6	5	41.6	10	83.3
MIDDLESEX	25	25	5	20.0	5	20.0	10	40.0
MONMOUTH (PART OF)	49	49	9	23.5	15	30.6	26	53.1
MORRIS	38	38	9	23.7	7	18.4	16	42.1
PASSAIC	16	16	6	37.5	4	25.0	10	62.5
SOMERSET	20	20	9	46.4	9	43.6	18	90.0
UNION	20	20	12	60.0	6	30.0	18	90.0
TOTAL STATE OF N.J.	274	274	95	34.7	87	31.8	182	66.4
FAIRFIELD (PART OF)	18	18	9	50.0	5	27.8	14	77.8
TOTAL FOR REGION	472	495	190	40.3	161	32.5	351	70.9

ZONING PROGRESS
NEW YORK REGION
STATUS IN 1930 AND 1940

MAY 1942

REGIONAL PLAN ASSOCIATION, Inc., NEW YORK

FIGURE 1

Scale in Miles
0 5 10 15

MUNICIPAL AREAS ZONED

ORDINANCE ENACTED BEFORE 1930

ORDINANCE ENACTED 1930-1940

NOTE: Based on returns from annual questionnaires sent to municipalities.

now used in any other part of the Region.

From 1916 through 1939 there were 1,151 zoning amendments. Of these 271, or about one-fourth, were adopted in the last decade. By far the greater number of changes involved amendments in the zoning maps. Changes were particularly numerous from 1925 through 1927 when real estate activities were at their peak.[1]

The most extensive revisions in the original use maps were the establishment of a retail district on April 18, 1929, and the extensive revision in residential and business district boundaries on the West Side of Manhattan in 1936. The extent of these changes are indicated in Figure 3, which covers the eleven-year period rather than the ten-year period used in illustrating the areas

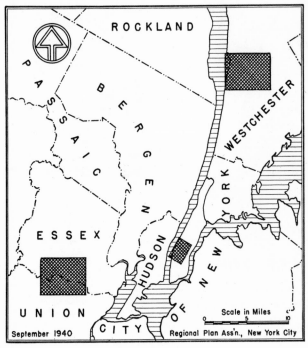

FIGURE 2
KEY TO SAMPLE AREAS STUDIED

selected outside of New York City, in order to show the extent of the change involved in establishing the retail district.

This new type of district was later refined by placing a very small section of it in a "restricted retail district," in which the construction of theaters, public dance halls and bus stations and the selling of automobiles on open lots are prohibited.

Many other changes have been made in the use maps since the establishment of the City Planning Commission in 1938,[2] both on its own initiative and through its

[1] Annual statistics are given in ANNUAL REPORT OF THE CITY PLANNING COMMISSION AND DEPARTMENT OF CITY PLANNING, THE CITY OF NEW YORK, 1939, page 74.
[2] See Information Bulletin No. 43, "Need for Rezoning Found in New York and Its Environs," October 31, 1938, page 9.

encouragement to other public departments and private agencies. The extent of these revisions, as compared with those made previously, is shown by a comparison prepared by the Commission's staff of the changes made by the Board of Estimate in 1927, the year when the largest number of changes in the City's history were made, and the changes effective in 1938, the first year the Commission was in existence. In 1927 there were 163 amendments covering a total of 2,403 acres; in 1938 there were 50 amendments covering 11,456 acres, or nearly five times the area affected by the larger number of changes in the earlier year.

Among the first changes initiated by the City Planning Commission was the establishment of a "G" district on the area maps wherein no dwelling may be erected other than for occupancy by a single family. Until the establishment of this district a multi-family dwelling could be constructed in any part of New York City, provided it conformed with height and area restrictions applicable to its site and to the Multiple Dwelling Law.

The new regulations of the recently amended Zoning Resolution of June 28, 1940, already referred to, provide for four new use districts for business and industry, but no areas were placed in such districts. The intention was to permit a more desirable separation of these uses than were provided for in the former Resolution. A brief summary of the regulations for these new districts is as follows:

Local Retail.—This provides a district in which retail stores would be restricted to ground floor occupancy. Regulations that govern uses in retail districts are applicable, except that manufacturing is excluded and no building may be built or altered if its upper story uses are intended for other than residential use.
Business–1 and Retail–1.—The same regulations apply in these districts as in business and retail districts, except that the new provisions limiting advertising and business signs are not in effect in these districts.
Manufacturing.—In this district 75 per cent of the total floor area of a building may be used for manufacturing purposes. The intent is to provide a zone intermediate between unrestricted and business districts, intended primarily for light industry.

New area districts were also established and were designated as D-1, E-1, and F-1 districts, respectively. While they would appear only on the area maps, they would be applied to areas zoned for residence on the use maps, and the regulations are designed to promote single-family row or group houses in D-1 districts; single-family twin or duplex houses in E-1 districts, and low density garden apartments in the F-1 districts. The control will be exercised largely through bulk limitations which are described in the discussion of density on page 10.

Additional amendments proposed by the City Planning Commission, but rejected by the Board of Esti-

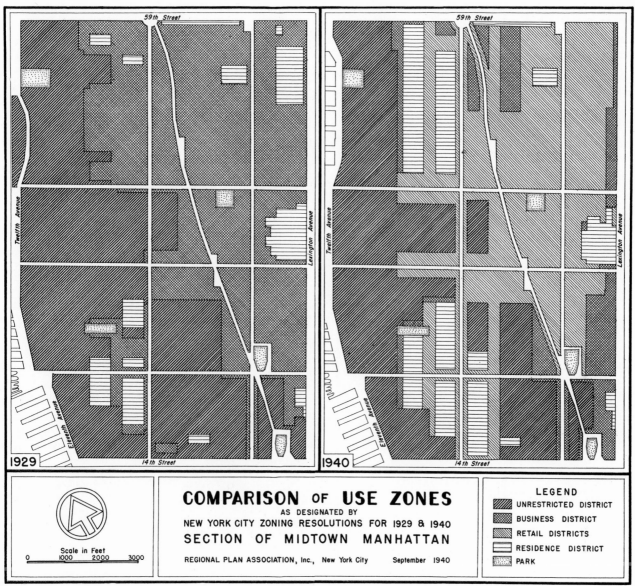

COMPARISON OF USE ZONES
AS DESIGNATED BY
NEW YORK CITY ZONING RESOLUTIONS FOR 1929 & 1940
SECTION OF MIDTOWN MANHATTAN
REGIONAL PLAN ASSOCIATION, Inc., New York City   September 1940

LEGEND
UNRESTRICTED DISTRICT
BUSINESS DISTRICT
RETAIL DISTRICTS
RESIDENCE DISTRICT
PARK

Scale in Feet
0   1000   2000   3000

FIGURE 3

mate, involved retroactive provisions in connection with garages, gasoline service stations and advertising signs. These uses, where non-conforming under the amended Resolution, would have been placed on a temporary permit basis, to be renewed every two years in the case of an advertising sign, every five years in the case of a gasoline filling station, and every ten years in the case of a garage. The Regional Plan Association urged the deletion of these provisions in regard to garages and gasoline filling stations, as recommended in the minority report of the City Planning Commission, and the adoption of the alternative provisions recommended in the minority report and incorporated by the Board of Estimate in the adopted Resolution.

These adopted provisions established the principle that existing uses of land for garages and gasoline ser-

vice stations which are non-conforming under the Resolution as amended may be terminated by the Board of Standards and Appeals, if, after a public hearing, said Board shall determine that such a use is a "hazard to life, health or the general welfare." Said Board, in making its decision, must however, also give due consideration to the investment involved. Any public agency, department head, or public institution may petition the Board of Standards and Appeals to terminate such an existing use, giving the reasons therefor.

The new use provisions adopted, together with other changes discussed hereafter, correct many of the basic defects in the 1916 Resolution. They also recognize present-day problems of city growth and social changes. Together they constitute a basis around which a comprehensive redistricting of the City should take place.

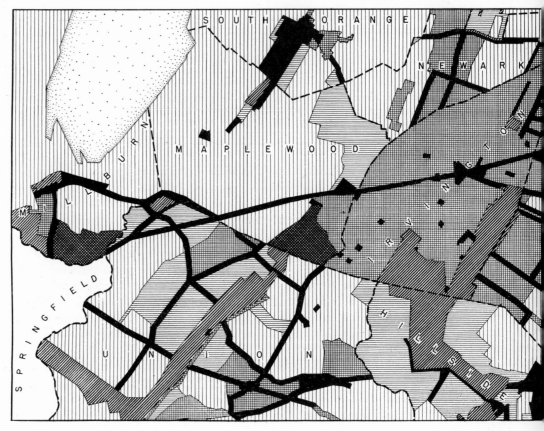

COMPARISON OF
USE ZONING
1930 AND 1940
SUBURBAN AREAS IN
THE NEW YORK REGION

REGIONAL PLAN ASS'N., Inc.
New York   September 1940

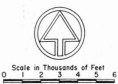

Scale in Thousands of Feet
0   1   2   3   4   5   6

1930
SECTION OF
WESTCHESTER
COUNTY

1930
SECTION OF
ESSEX & UNION
COUNTIES

FIGURE 4
(1930 Conditions)

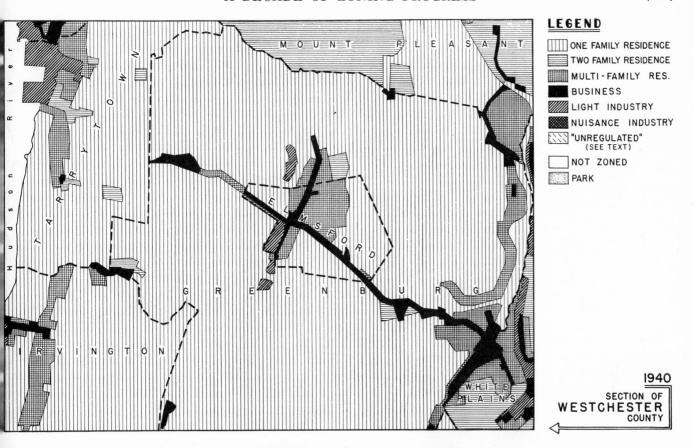

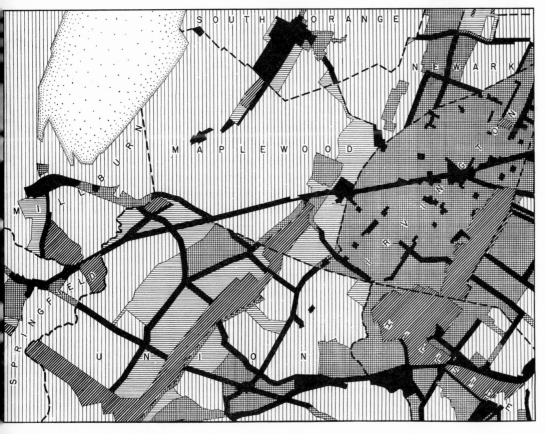

LEGEND

⬚ ONE FAMILY RESIDENCE
⬚ TWO FAMILY RESIDENCE
⬚ MULTI-FAMILY RES.
■ BUSINESS
▨ LIGHT INDUSTRY
▨ NUISANCE INDUSTRY
▨ "UNREGULATED"
   (SEE TEXT)
□ NOT ZONED
⬚ PARK

1940
SECTION OF
WESTCHESTER
COUNTY

1940
SECTION OF
ESSEX & UNION
COUNTIES

FIGURE 4
(1940 Conditions)

In the Environs

The six classifications of use zones, already referred to, shown on the maps in Figure 4, which illustrate typical trends in the environs during the decade 1930 to 1940, are based on the following subdivision of uses:

Single-Family.—Single-family dwellings, religious, educational and charitable institutions, clubs if not conducted for gain, home occupations such as dressmaking and millinery if conducted by residents, and professional offices.

Two-Family.—Two-family and single-family dwellings, clubs conducted for gain, and usually hospitals, sanitariums, hotels, boarding and rooming houses.

Multi-Family.—Apartment houses, garden apartments and tenements.

Business.—Retail business and small-scale industrial uses which are incidental to a business or facilitate convenient supplies for nearby residential districts.

Industry.—Commercial and industrial uses, but excluding such industries as might be detrimental to health or safety.[1]

Nuisance Industry.—Areas which permit any lawful type of use without regard to its effect upon health or safety.

Unzoned.—Areas not having zoning regulations.

The first classification is essentially for one-family dwellings and no other types of dwellings are permitted therein; the second classification, where two-family dwellings are also permitted, is often used for buffer zones between business or apartment zones and the more attractive residential areas. There has also been a tendency to place some of the older single-family areas in this second classification as land values have increased with urban growth. Regulations governing these districts are not uniform and lot sizes vary according to the locality. Multi-family and commercial districts are frequently subdivided in the zoning ordinance so as to permit varying degrees of intensity of land occupancy or use.

A general inspection of the maps in Figure 4, showing trends in two typical areas, will reveal clearly the influence of existing ways of communication. It is interesting to note that business districts are not confined to central locations of communities. The predominance of "shoe-string" business districts is due partly to overzoning and, to a lesser extent, to the poor street arrangement in the central business areas. Recent zoning revisions have corrected this condition to a small degree, but both areas are suggestive of the need for a more efficient organization of a use pattern which should be related to a physical development plan.

A statistical summary of the zoned use districts, as shown on the maps of typical areas, is given in the following table:

PROPORTION OF VARIOUS USE DISTRICTS, AS ZONED IN 1930 AND 1940 IN TWO TYPICAL SUBURBAN AREAS, EXPRESSED AS PERCENTAGE OF TOTAL AREA

Zoned use districts, as classified in this study	In typical suburban residential area[1]		In typical suburban manufacturing area[2]	
	1930	1940	1930	1940
Single-family	53.0%	77.2%	42.8%	48.9%
Two-family	3.8	6.4	12.7	8.5
Multi-family	12.3	10.5	19.3	22.2
Business	4.9	3.7	9.3	11.2
Industry	1.1	2.2	9.1	9.2
Nuisance industry	0.2	0.0	2.0	0.0
Unzoned	24.7	0.0	4.8	0.0
Total	100%	100%	100%	100%

[1] Village of Elmsford and parts of the following municipalities: City of White Plains; towns of Greenburgh, Mount Pleasant and North Castle; villages of Irvington, North Tarrytown, Tarrytown and Scarsdale.

[2] Township of Maplewood and parts of the following municipalities: cities of East Orange and Newark; Town of Irvington; townships of Hillside, Millburn, Springfield and Union; Village of South Orange.

Residential Areas.—Tendencies of use zoning in suburban residential communities were found to be fairly consistent. A section of central Westchester County has been selected to illustrate typical trends in these types of communities. The representative area contains relatively small amounts of business and industrial zones which were primarily laid out to provide for local shopping and manufacture.

Of the nine communities, or parts of same, included in the sample area, two have adopted zoning and four have extensively revised their use pattern since 1930. Excluding the newly zoned communities, there has been a reduction in the extent of districts set aside for the less restricted uses, as can be seen by comparing the maps in the upper part of Figure 4. A summation of zoned uses in the area for the periods under review is given on a percentage basis in the table above.

As a whole, single-family districts have gained and multi-family districts have decreased in size. The large area of two-family zone in the Town of Mount Pleasant in 1940, replacing what was formerly allotted to single-family use, is an exception to the general trend. The Westchester County Farm and a large New York City institution occupy a large portion of this particular district. Their influence on immediately surrounding land is responsible for this change.

The large area in the Village of Irvington, shown as "unregulated" in 1930, is a literal interpretation of its ordinance at that time which read:

"Districts 'B', 'C' and 'F' are so situated and subject to such conditions that the public health and general welfare of the community are deemed to require no protection."

These districts were specified as residential with no other form of regulation except the exclusion of commercial uses. The weakness of this type of use zoning is obvious in that it permits an owner to develop his property without regard to desirable standards. This

---

[1] The industries most often excluded are the following: manufacture or storage of gas or explosive materials; manufacture of celluloid, lamp black, glue, sizing, gelatine, oil cloth or linoleum; the distillation of coal, wood or bones; slaughtering of animals. The types of industry usually excluded from "light industrial zones" depend upon local opinions. A uniform distinction between light and heavy industrial uses has not manifested itself to date.

particular village has since rezoned to provide a more positive method of regulation.

Business districts have been drastically reduced in the Town of Greenburgh. On the other hand, the villages of Elmsford and Irvington have restricted practically all of their former industrial zones to business uses. Use districts for nuisance industry have been completely eliminated in all of the communities encompassed in this area. Other 1930 industrial zones have also been reduced in area, although some additional ones have been established in newly zoned communities.

With respect to general trends for suburban residential areas of the Region, there is a marked tendency toward increasing single-family districts with the intent of maintaining low population densities. This is confirmed by a current scaling down of commercial and multi-family zones in practically all suburban residential communities; also by the application of more stringent density regulations in these districts, to be discussed in more detail in a later section of this Chapter.

Manufacturing Areas.—Typical tendencies of use zoning in industrial communities and adjacent surroundings are illustrated on the maps in the lower part of Figure 4. This section lies in Essex and Union counties, New Jersey, and is flanked on the east by the cities of Newark and Elizabeth. A small part of the former city is included. Most of the communities in the area are highly industrialized and more densely populated than the representative area in Westchester County.

Four of the nine communities, or parts of same, included in this area, have extensively revised their use patterns during the past ten years; one has adopted zoning for the first time. The tendencies of use revisions in this and other similar parts of the Region have been to increase business and multi-family use zones. The evils of overzoning have been partly recognized, as indicated by the reduction of industrial districts and the prohibition of nuisance industry. The percentages of the total area for the various zoned uses in 1930 and 1940 are given in the table on page 8.

Rezoning in the Town of Irvington and the Township of Hillside are responsible for the increase in business and multi-family use zones. The rates of population growth for these communities between 1920 and 1930 amounted to 122 per cent and 235 per cent, respectively. The momentum of this exceptional growth undoubtedly carried on for a period after 1930 and is responsible for the expansion of the above use zones. The other two communities that revised their districts are of a residential character and the changes made

are a result of tendencies similar to those pointed out in the Westchester County area.

Trends for industrial communities of the Region have not as yet indicated a conclusive movement toward a reduction in the area, and hence the population capacity, of multi-family zones or any substantial reduction in the area of business districts. High land values established and sanctioned by overzoning are a controlling factor in any such movement. The nation-wide diminishing rate of population growth revealed by the 1940 census forecasts the need for immediately relating use zoning to the needs of a less dynamic future.

TRENDS IN PROVISIONS OF ZONING ORDINANCES

The record of zoning in its early days indicated that ordinances were frequently passed only to be overruled by the courts. Probably the most significant single trend of advance in recent years is the courts' increasing respect for zoning and sympathy with its aims; regulations considered radical a comparatively few years ago are today regarded as legitimate uses of the police power under which zoning operates. In addition, increasing public understanding of the aims and advantages of zoning has gradually made it easier to have ordinances adopted and get more efficient restrictions.

Innovations consistent with principles of sound city planning have been incorporated in several zoning ordinances throughout the Region. Some of the contributions of New York City's revised Zoning Resolution are its provisions to: facilitate off-street loading of trucks; protect row or group housing from denser forms of residential development; facilitate large-scale housing projects; and provide for the safe operation of publicly owned airports.

In general, types of zoning ordinances have continued more or less along the same lines as summarized in an earlier report.[1] Before 1930 there was a distinct tendency for the limitations set by zoning to be unnecessarily liberal due to its problematical status. For example, the density of building possible under most of the older ordinances provides for a population that can never be realized. At the same time, areas allotted to commercial uses are far in excess of even the most optimistic growth. These fallacies have gradually been recognized and today there is a marked desire on the part of zoning officials to strengthen and correct their standards. The majority of ordinances enacted since 1930 reflect this attitude. Several trends in this tightening-up process and progressive viewpoint are worthy of separate discussion.

[1] See FROM PLAN TO REALITY, 1933, page 102.

Densities

Significant among other advances of zoning is a growing tendency to prevent, by various methods of controlling density, the overcrowding of land with buildings. In general, zoning ordinances adopted before 1930, controlled population density only indirectly, by area and height standards. Practically all ordinances adopted since then contain provisions for direct control. Many municipalities in the Region have revised their ordinances during the past few years to increase the stringency of such provisions and to curtail building bulk in both apartment and commercial districts.

To what extent earlier studies[1] of the Regional Plan are responsible for this movement or have contributed to the public understanding of the problem cannot be determined. Regardless of the motivating cause, it is one of the most encouraging trends in the steady evolution of zoning.

Limited space permits presentation herein of only a few examples of improved density regulations. Those selected are representative of tendencies in all parts of the Region.

Original zoning in the Town of Hempstead, Long Island, adopted in 1931, permitted a density of 70 families per acre in business and industrial districts. Subsequent revisions lowered this figure to 40 families in both districts. In 1939 the Village of Irvington, N. Y., arbitrarily lowered the maximum height of buildings permitted in apartment districts from six stories to three and one-half stories.

The land-per-family requirement in residential districts of suburban communities has continued to increase in varying degrees. In connection with the general trend toward a lower population density per unit of land, it is interesting to note that many suburban communities, particularly in northern New Jersey, have established setbacks and side yard requirements stringent enough to discourage cheap single-family houses. It is claimed that cheap houses on small lots are not self-supporting and place heavier burdens on the more substantial types of development. Drastic area revisions of the zoning ordinances in the communities of Alpine, Harrington Park, Haworth, Closter and Demarest in Bergen County, have been based on this premise.

Multi-family zones in several suburban communities in New Jersey have been made subject to greater yard and height requirements. These call for front and side yards equal to or greater than those required for single-family houses. In these cases building height has also been limited to two and one-half stories, coverage to 25 per cent and the density of population maintained the same as in single-family districts.

New York City.—As mentioned on page 4, New York City has established a density control through bulk limitations set up in its revised Zoning Resolution. This was done by stipulating a maximum ratio between the gross floor area of a building and the area of the lot on which it is located, such requirements to be uniform throughout a district shown on the area map. (New York City, as already explained, has three sets of maps and district boundaries; one for use, one for height and one for area.) The bulk limitation was applied, however, only to three types of area districts: the E and F districts and a newly established F-1 District. In each case they were aimed at controlling apartments which might be built adjacent to single-family homes in these districts. The ratios established were: the gross floor area shall not exceed 1.9 times the area of an interior lot and 2.5 times the area of a corner lot in the E District; 1.6 times the area of an interior lot and 1.9 times the area of a corner lot in the F District; and 0.75 times the area of any lot in the F-1 District.

The Regional Plan Association strongly endorsed this new type of regulation although it stated that it would like to see lower ratios established and the same type of regulation extended to other types of areas, particularly the C and D districts where apartment buildings now crowd the land far more intensively than there is any occasion for and where a continuation of the same type of buildings will cause future blighted areas.[1]

This type of regulation is similar to one proposed in 1936 by a Joint Committee of the Mayor's Committee on City Planning and the City Club of New York, where ratios were considered for business as well as residential districts. The ratios recommended to this committee by a member of the Association's staff started with a maximum gross floor area of 12 times the area of the lot in the A Districts where the skyscrapers are now located.[2]

The three new area districts already referred to on page 4 are designed to encourage and protect specific types of development having relatively low population densities. In D-1 Districts there is no explicit limitation on the number of single-family row houses that

---

[1] See Information Bulletin No. 18, "Present Extent and Future Needs of Land for Residential Development," May 14, 1934, and Regional Plan, Volume II, THE BUILDING OF THE CITY, page 258.

[1] The Association's recommendations, as submitted at the hearings before the City Planning Commission, called for the following maximum gross floor areas, without distinction as to interior and corner lots: 3.0 times the area of the lot in C Districts; 2.0 times in D Districts; 1.5 times in E Districts; 1.0 times in F Districts; and 0.5 times in F-1 Districts.
[2] See Information Bulletin No. 43, October 31, 1938, page 7.

can be built together but a graduated side yard requirement will tend to limit the number of units to desirable
proportions.

Regulations of E-1 Districts limit occupancy to a
single family, as in the previously established G Districts, but are less stringent than those of the latter.
Two attached single-family dwellings are permitted
and a minimum sum of 12 feet are required for side
yards.

Considerable flexibility is permitted in the regulations governing buildings in F-1 Districts. In effect a
three-story building is limited to 25 per cent coverage
but a six-story building could have only about 12 per
cent coverage, with other combinations in proportion.

Billboard and Sign Control

Billboards and advertising signs are already success-
fully regulated in residential districts by practically all
zoning ordinances. However, in business and industrial
districts otherwise attractive streets or highways are
often utterly spoiled by flagrant billboards and roof
signs. Some of the more recent zoning ordinances have
regulated this practice by limiting the size of billboards
and permitting their location only in certain areas.
Other forms of "outdoor advertising," such as loud
speakers and floodlighting, have been recognized in
several communities as public annoyances. In these
communities the use of the above appliances is prohibited in all but industrial zones.

Without doubt overhanging street signs give a business district a tawdry atmosphere. There are so many
signs on the average business street that they tend to
obscure each other at night and become a conglomerate
glare of light, defeating the purpose for which they
were erected. A movement to correct this condition can
be traced throughout the Region. In general, restrictions call for a reasonable relationship between the area
of the sign and the building facade. Projection over the
public street is drastically limited so that in most instances it is practical to erect only signs flat against the
building.

Notable examples of the latter type of practice are
found along Fifth and Madison Avenues in New York
City where curtailment of street signs is secured not
by zoning but by voluntary cooperation of property
owners. The example of these world renowned shopping
thoroughfares should be sufficient inducement for the
reform of shopping streets in smaller communities. Of
the numerous suburban shopping districts where regulation of overhanging street signs have been particularly effective, Garden City, Long Island, and Upper
Montclair, N. J., offer convincing testimony of the prac-

ticability of such control. In both communities store
owners have pronounced such regulation a help rather
than a hindrance to business.

In New York City the new Zoning Resolution makes
a distinction between billboards and signs advertising
a business conducted on the premises. It prohibits the
former entirely and limits the latter, in both size and
type, in all business, retail and local retail districts.
The City Planning Commission recognized that there
are certain areas in the city, such as the Times Square
theater district, where these controls of signs are
neither desirable nor practicable. There were, therefore, established in the new Resolution two new types
of business districts, already referred to and designated
as Business-1 and Retail-1 districts, in which these
restrictions shall not apply.[1]

States and the Federal government are making, or
aiding in, the tremendous investments of public improvements throughout the Region. Protection of these
from abuses of billboard practices is imperative if
natural amenities are to be preserved and the public
interest safeguarded. In the case of state highways and
parkways zoning has proved "spotty."

In the first place, the improvement usually passes
through some municipalities that have not adopted zoning ordinances and is therefore unprotected. Even
where there is zoning the local community is very often
so sensitive to the lure of an immediate increase in tax
rateables that it overzones for business with approximately the same result as no zoning. In the case of
parkways in Westchester and Nassau counties and New
York City the agencies responsible for them have been
active in persuading the localities through which the
improvements pass to adopt adequate zoning restrictions in the districts adjacent to the right-of-way.

Some broader form of regulation such as the Act[2]
proposed by a committee composed of state and local
officials of New York and various civic organizations is
desirable. Such legislation was introduced in the 1939
New York Legislature but failed of adoption.

New York City has sought to prevent the continuation of indiscriminate placing of billboards in relation
to public improvements. It has incorporated in its Zoning Resolution a provision to regulate this practice
which stipulates:

"No advertising sign shall hereafter be erected or structurally

---

1 On Ocotber 2, 1940, the City Planning Commission adopted a report
approving the establishment of both Business-1 and Retail-1 districts in
the vicinity of Times Square and arranging for later hearings on enlarge-
ments of these new districts.

2 For provisions of the Act see "The Billboard, a Blot on Nature and
a Parasite on Public Improvements," January 2, 1939, by a Committee
composed of Superintendent of Public Works, State of New York; Commissioner of Parks, City of New York; Conservation Commissioner, State
of New York; Chairman, New York City Planning Commission; and with
the cooperation of the New York Roadside Improvement and Safety
Committee.

altered in any use district within 200 feet of a highway designated by the City Planning Commission as an express highway to which the provision of this section shall apply or within 200 feet of a public park of one-half acre or more in area, if within view of such highway or park."

Off-Street Parking of Automobiles

While the problem of providing off-street facilities for the parking of automobiles and for the loading and unloading of trucks involves other methods of approach, much has been done to remedy this situation through the use of zoning. It occurs both in multi-family residential and in business districts and can best be discussed under these headings.

In Multi-Family Districts.—Among the many factors affecting the success of storage facilities designed for the cars of tenants in multi-family buildings, convenience and economy are perhaps dominant. If the garage or parking space is in an out-of-the-way location, the tenant will tend to use the street space nearest to his entrance, for the most of the daytime at least. If the garage space is expensive and an apartment may be rented without taking such space, the tenant will tend to use the street space day and night except perhaps in midwinter, if he is permitted to do so.

The mere provision of off-street parking space is thus no guarantee that the streets will remain clear for moving vehicles, but if reasonable facilities are provided it would be feasible to enforce parking restrictions which would facilitate traffic movement. Thus zoning and traffic relief are closely related in apartment areas.

Several of the suburban communities in the Region have permitted garages for tenants to be constructed as accessory buildings on a lot used for a multi-family dwelling but such a permissive regulation was not put into the New York City Zoning Resolution until the revisions of June 28, 1940 were adopted.

Within recent years there has been a very definite trend to make such provisions compulsory instead of merely permissive. '

Among the more recent examples are the villages of Hempstead and Valley Stream, on Long Island; Greenwich, in Connecticut; and New Rochelle, in Westchester County. The two Long Island communities require parking and storage facilities for a number of cars equal to three-fourths of the number of families for which the buildings are designed. The Greenwich ordinance calls for a storage capacity of two-thirds of the number of families, and New Rochelle for one-half the number of families. The New Rochelle provisions

for the location of such garages state that all such garages shall be constructed and located within the building, beneath the side or rear yards or courts, or in a separate building, in each case conforming with certain specifications.

In most cases the maximum capacity of the storage space must not exceed space for one car for each family.

In Central Business Districts.—The primary effort in central business districts has been to require facilities for short time parking for patrons and for the loading and unloading of trucks. This can most readily be done in connection with the establishment of new neighborhood shopping districts but is also justified in established business centers.

Among the former type of regulations is a provision in the ordinance of the Town of Montclair, N. J. that in all new business zones there should be a rear service lane provided on each lot for off-street loading and unloading of vehicles and with direct access from a public street. The New Rochelle ordinance, already referred to, includes the following provision for business districts:

"All loft buildings, department stores, retail and wholesale food markets or stores, warehouses or supply houses erected after the date of adoption of this Ordinance shall provide one unloading berth for motor vehicles of 200 square feet for each 8,000 square feet of gross floor area devoted to such purposes. This may be provided either within the building or on open space on the same lot and the minimum clear height of such space, including access to it from the street, shall be 14 feet. This provision shall not apply to any building with less than 8,000 square feet of gross floor devoted to such purposes."

Another example of a smaller community is the Village of Dobbs Ferry, in Westchester County, which recently adopted regulations requiring off-street parking space on the premises, or on other nearby premises, for customers and employees in certain types of new business buildings.

The revised Zoning Resolution of New York City has a comprehensive requirement for loading space in new or enlarged buildings to be used for manufacture, storage, or goods display, or for a department store, hotel or hospital. Following closely recommendations made to the Board of Estimate and Apportionment some years ago by the Merchants' Association of New York, it requires one truck loading or unloading berth for each 25,000 square feet of gross floor area arranged, intended or designed for such uses. Direct access from the loading space to a public street is required. Buildings having less than 25,000 square feet of floor area are exempted from these provisions.

VI. PROGRESS AND PROBLEMS OF PLANNING AGENCIES

Planning as a means of guiding community development has experienced a swiftly changing environment, passing from prosperity through depression to wartime. Evolutionary changes induced by the need for adaptation are apparent in a review of progress of planning agencies in the Region in the 1937-1941 period. Some agencies have increased in vigor, new agencies and functions have appeared, while planning in other instances has withered into inactivity.[1]

There are now more official planning boards than five years ago, more executive agencies of government which understand and apply the planning method, more general interest in planning, and more recognition in particular that, for our larger cities, the alternative to planned rejuvenation is decay. Some planning boards have carried out thorough, realistic planning jobs. On the other hand, there is only a bare handful of such active agencies, although they are needed in dozens of the Region's cities. Many millions spent on public improvements and new private building have been entirely without benefit of guidance by a planned, overall community policy. Moreover, official planning boards in general have made a poor response to the challenge of defense and war needs. It is a mixed record, revealing progress but providing scant grounds for complacency.

There has been a significant shift in the center of gravity of planning work from the local community toward the county, state and Nation. Multiplication of Federal agencies has been the dominant governmental development of the period. Increasing numbers of local, state and regional branches of these agencies have set up shop in the Region, touching upon the life of the metropolis at an increasing number of points. Well staffed with statistical and research personnel—in Washington, if not locally—and conscious of the critical need of competent administration and policy making, these agencies have widely adopted and applied the planning approach.

In units of local government within the Region, a number of new planning boards were established, most of them in New Jersey and Nassau County. Many local planning agencies, however, including relatively new ones, have lapsed into inactivity. And the birth rate of planning boards must be partially discounted in view of a phenomenon unfamiliar to the field—a death rate; for the slumbers of at least three boards in the Region have been sanctified by official dissolution in recent years.

The establishment of the New York City Planning Commission and Department of Planning in 1938, and its subsequent intensive work, is the greatest single planning development in the Region in the five-year period. But the majority of the Region's cities of over 20,000 population have no planning agency at all and only a few have planning staffs at work.

Planning at the neighborhood level made a measure of concrete progress under the auspices of the United States Housing Authority in the projects of local housing authorities, and through the work of the Federal Housing Administration with private developers. The future may bring greater accomplishment; recent state legislation in New York envisions concerted action by public officials and private investment institutions in which the neighborhood will be the basic unit in the redevelopment of blighted urban areas in the post-war period.

The stresses and swift changes accompanying the emergence of a war economy have placed a premium on the availability of basic local data in organized and related form, and on the ability of public officials of all government units to make quick, sound decisions based on these data. This need, and the demand for formulation of public works budgets and schedules to cushion post-war depression, constitute a challenge to planning agencies in the coming period. The stakes are survival and an opportunity for vital service.

STATE PLANNING

Possibly the most significant trend in the work of the three official state planning agencies in the Region —the New York State Division of Commerce, the New Jersey State Planning Board, and the Connecticut State Development Commission—has been the increased emphasis on planning to strengthen the basic economic activities of their respective areas. The prolonged depression and increased awareness of the threat of industrial decentralization and migration have underscored the point that an area's productivity and prosperity cannot be taken for granted, but must be sustained and fortified against competing influences by planned action of the commonwealth.

This trend was clearly delineated in changes in the actual organizational framework in New York State and Connecticut, where planning, previously set up as a separate function, was consolidated into agencies expressly concerned with the overall objective of increased economic strength. The Connecticut State Development Commission in 1939 took over the work of the former Connecticut State Planning Board, and in

---

[1] See FROM PLAN TO REALITY, TWO (1938), published by Regional Plan Association, Inc., for a review of planning progress through 1937.

1941 the New York State Planning Council was abolished and a new Division of Commerce was established; the former Division of Planning was reorganized as a bureau of the new agency.

As the defense and war emergencies have developed, the state planning work in New York has emphasized the industrial adjustments of the war production program. The Bureau of Planning has prepared an industrial directory of the state, an inventory of idle plant and idle machine tool facilities, and a statistical analysis of recent trends in the state's manufacturing industries as compared with other states. Earlier in the period under review, the former State Division of Planning conducted extensive studies, assembling general basic data covering water resources, land use, population, and aviation development, and giving special attention to studies of premature land subdivision, and local and regional planning activities.

Increased concern with economic activity is also reflected in the work of the New Jersey State Planning Board, which has studied intra-state regional trends of industry and population, and has been developing an inventory of industries and a check on industrial movement. This work is part of a program aiming toward a general development plan, which has also involved studies of parks and public lands, local government airports and airways, and premature subdivision. In 1941 Governor Edison requested the board to ready the state development plan as a basis for preparing post-war public works.

In 1942, the New Jersey Board was assigned the data-gathering and mapping job on war industry commutation, to enable the state's War Transportation Committee to make adjustments to the rubber shortage. Recent activities, in which the board is keying in more closely with the work of other state departments, give grounds for hope for increase over the low appropriations which for several years handicapped the agency with inadequacy of staff and quarters.

Work of the Connecticut State Development Commission has included development studies of mineral resources, and preparation of an industrial plant inventory and an atlas of industrial sites. The last two projects were intensified in response to the demands of swiftly expanding war industries in the state.

The Regional Plan Association was instrumental in organizing state federations of official planning boards, in New York in 1937, and in New Jersey in 1939, and is continuing cooperation with their work to foster planning interest and effort among local boards through meetings and monthly publications. The New York Federation has been conducting an annual Municipal Training School for planning and zoning officials in cooperation with other interested state agencies.

The New Jersey State Chamber of Commerce, heading an effort for parkway legislation, was assisted by the New Jersey Federation and the Association in mobilizing the support of other civic groups. The Association was represented on a committee of the New Jersey Federation which recently initiated a program to draft and push urban redevelopment legislation.

COUNTY PLANNING

Recent population growth has been swift in several of the Region's suburban areas, as in Bergen and Nassau counties. Many problems such as water supply and sanitation, which have previously been approached from the local angle in suburban areas, now require the formulation of development programs along the more logical lines of drainage basins. Wherever residential expansion assumes a metropolitan character, local boundaries lose much of their original signifi-

cance, and need develops for coordinated solution of joint problems of groups of municipalities which grow into each other. Where county planning has shown vitality, this may be attributed largely to its strategic position to effect such coordination. Once established, it can also contribute greatly to the strength of planning in small localities which are enabled to bypass their own financial limitations by turning to the county agency for basic data and expert technical assistance.

In practice, although many counties made headway in the fact-gathering stage of the planning job, very few have been able thus far to climb to the more important level of digging out the significance of the gathered facts and deriving realistic development objectives to guide county and municipal expenditures. On the other hand, those few agencies which have carried the job forward have demonstrated strongly the usefulness of the county-wide planning approach.

The *Bergen* County Planning Board is outstanding in point of volume and character of actual planning work carried through. Utilizing the services of the Association's technical staff, this board has followed up the initial work of mapping and fact finding with studies of land subdivision, water supply, sanitation, zoning, transportation, and population. This has been accompanied by a steady effort to place results of the board's work before the public through an organized program of special reports, pamphlets, news releases, and exhibits, and through cooperation with the municipal governments of the county. The highway, park and parkway phases of the master plan have been adopted by the Planning Board and the official map has been adopted by the Board of Chosen Freeholders.

Rockland County's Planning Board, getting under way somewhat later than its neighbor to the south, has worked on similar lines, aiming toward formulation of a master plan. County planning boards have been appointed in Westchester, Morris, and Passaic counties since 1937. In *Westchester* the planning commission's work has included preparation of a capital budget for the county. The *Morris* County Planning Board cooperated with the Association in the publication in 1939 of a booklet on "Morris County and the Regional Plan," forming one of the Association's series of such booklets. The *Passaic* County Planning Board has recently launched studies toward a master plan with the aim of formulating a sound post-war public works program. The *Fairfield* County Planning Association and the *Orange* County Planning Board have also continued in active service.

On the other side of the ledger must be reckoned a number of counties where planning activity has stalled. In Union, Essex, Somerset, and Putnam counties, the valuable data assembled in WPA planning projects have gathered dust for lack of a permanent agency to analyze them and derive appropriate lines of public policy. In Middlesex and Dutchess counties, planning boards were appointed and gathered basic data under WPA projects but no line of action was developed and the Middlesex board was disbanded at the end of 1940 and the Dutchess board has recently become inactive. In still other counties, the autonomous character of planning boards as typically proposed has alienated the support of county officials and executives, who have objected to the creation of what they assumed would become a competing policy-making body. In Nassau County, which is building up so fast that development problems are rapidly outgrowing municipal boundaries, a county planning board with extensive powers was provided for in the new county charter adopted in 1938, but the board has not yet been appointed.

CITY OF NEW YORK
CITY PLANNING COMMISSION
DEPARTMENT OF CITY PLANNING
MASTER PLAN
EXPRESS HIGHWAYS, PARKWAYS AND
MAJOR STREETS
PREPARED BY
DIVISION OF MASTER PLAN

NOTE: FOR SOUTH RICHMOND
SEE INSERT ABOVE

REPORT Nº 1974 ADOPTED JULY 16, 1941

Courtesy, New York City Planning Commission

FIGURE 1

LOCAL PLANNING

Major interest in local planning during the period under review has focussed on the New York City Planning Commission, which had just been established when the last volume of PLAN TO REALITY was published. Vested with broad powers, and incorporating the feature of full-time, paid commissioners, it has been looked to for the fullest demonstration of the potentialities of the semi-independent planning agency. The commission and the Department of City Planning by 1941 had a total personnel of 67 and a budget of $267,000. However, a great part of the energies of the department have been absorbed by relatively routine functions, such as mapping and zoning, which had been transferred to the department from other city agencies. Such divisions as those of Master Plan and of Capital and Assessable Improvements, vital to actual planning work, have been far from free of the pinch of budget limitations. Despite this, planning accomplishments have been substantial in volume, and they have been characterized by a clear grasp of the broad, difficult problems which face the metropolis in coming years.

Sections of the master plan were developed, and official adoption secured of those covering schools, hospitals, parks, highways, and areas for clearance, re-planning and low-rent housing. Proposed arterial highways are tied in with the scheme of the Regional Plan. The capital budgeting function of the commission has emerged as one of its most significant, for here it has wielded an implement for brass-tacks guidance of the city's development.

However, the commission's master plan of land use came a cropper, largely because it was published without sufficient preliminary understanding of its nature and purposes. Maps intended to illustrate general principles were confused with zoning maps. The plan, which aimed at a stabilized and more evenly and widely distributed residential population, raised issues which need much public discussion before they achieve general understanding. When the report came up for adoption the commission personnel, which had changed in the interim, brushed it aside in an understandable but perhaps excessive reaction. The net result was to create a cloud of confusion around the subject of land use planning which it will take some time to dispel.

Planning progress in the Region's municipalities outside New York City may be looked at in two ways, yielding radically different conclusions. If the establishment of planning boards *per se* is taken as an objective and as a measuring rod, local planning in the Region has moved ahead; from 1937 to 1941, 64 new planning boards were reported, against three which became inactive and were formally disbanded. Thus, of 495 municipal units on January 1, 1941, 204 had municipal planning agencies as compared with 143 reporting such agencies four years before. These statistics, compared with figures for 1929, are shown by counties in the accompanying table.

If, however, we take the point of view that active, staffed planning agencies are necessary for an adequate planning job, particularly in the satellite cities of the Region, progress to date has been disappointing. Of the six satellite cities in the Region with a population of over 100,000, only two—Yonkers and Bridgeport—had planning boards with 1941 appropriations to support full-time staff work. In 1940 Yonkers created a separate agency for industrial research and promotion, to which was diverted half of the appropriation formerly received by the planning commission. In two other of these six leading cities, Paterson and Elizabeth, industrial commissions rather than planning boards have been established in response to depression-time municipal problems.

The number of smaller municipalities in the Region which had 1941 planning appropriations of more than $1,500 was as follows: only Passaic of the eight cities with a population of between 50,000 and 100,000; only seven of the 35 municipalities with a population

STATUS OF MUNICIPAL PLANNING IN THE REGION,
JANUARY 1, 1929, 1937, 1941

County	Number of municipalities		Number of planning boards reported		
	1929	1937 and 1941	1929	1937	1941
NEW YORK STATE					
New York City (5 counties) . . .	1	1	0	1a	1
*Dutchess (Part of) .	6	6	0	0	0
Nassaub	36	68	10	25	42
*Orange (Part of) .	19	19	0	6	6
Putnam	9	9	0	1	1
*Rockland	15	16	0	1	4
*Suffolk	31	40	0	14	14
*Westchester	44	44	22	32	37
Total New York State	161	203	32	79	104
NEW JERSEY					
*Bergen	70	70	6	17	34
Essex	22	22	8	12	13
Hudson	12	12	1	0	1
Middlesex	25	25	2	4	8
Monmouth (Part of)	47	49	0	2	5
*Morris	34	38	0	4	8
*Passaic	16	16	2	3	3
Somerset	22	22	1	5	8
Union	20	20	5	8	11
Total New Jersey	268	274	25	55	91
CONNECTICUT					
Fairfieldc (Part of) .	19	18	4	9	9
Total Region . .	448	495	61	143	204

* County planning board, 1941. In the Region's 17 counties outside New York City, there were no official county planning boards in 1929, seven in 1937, and eight in 1941.
a Mayor's Committee on City Planning, succeeded in 1938 by City Planning Commission and Department, with an Advisory Planning Board in each borough.
b County planning board provided for in 1938 charter revision, but not established.
c Fairfield County Planning Association, unofficial, is active.

of between 20,000 and 50,000; and only four of the 51 with a population of between 10,000 and 20,000.

In total, of the Region's 100 municipalities outside New York City of more than 10,000 population, only 14 had 1941 appropriations sufficient to support full-time staff work. The picture is roughly the same in the smaller communities, where the actual figures are of less significance since unpaid boards with the help of staff informally borrowed from regular village departments in many cases carry on fruitful activity. But for cities of more than 10,000, it may fairly be stated that failure to secure staff appropriations indicates that planning boards are not making a significant contribution to the community's management and development—particularly in the current period when municipalities face complex, fast-changing difficulties.

The activity of local planning boards has, in general, not changed greatly in character in recent years, when the functions of government as a whole were changing and expanding a great deal. The planning idea was pioneered in an era of growth; its original philosophy was the orderly guidance of growth, and the curbing of the "wild horse of municipal expendi-

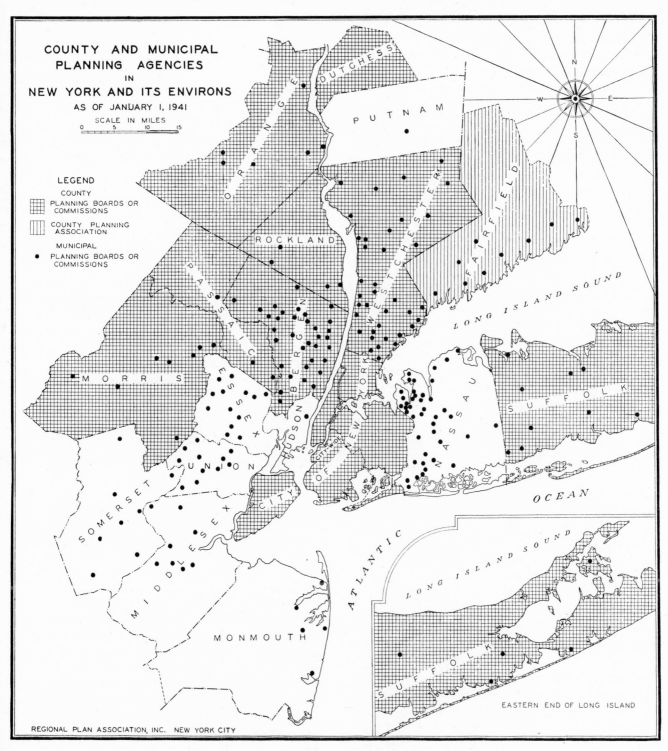

COUNTY AND MUNICIPAL
PLANNING AGENCIES
IN
NEW YORK AND ITS ENVIRONS
AS OF JANUARY 1, 1941

SCALE IN MILES
0   5   10   15

LEGEND
COUNTY
PLANNING BOARDS OR
COMMISSIONS
COUNTY PLANNING
ASSOCIATION
MUNICIPAL
PLANNING BOARDS OR
COMMISSIONS

REGIONAL PLAN ASSOCIATION, INC. NEW YORK CITY

EASTERN END OF LONG ISLAND

FIGURE 2

ture." In the past ten years, when the "wild horse" has been sick, only a few planning boards have seen the need to rethink their function, and to become diagnosticians coordinating the host of new remedial government functions which seek to promote industrial stability, alleviate social insecurity, and exterminate urban blight. Many planning agencies have stayed within the older boundaries of planning land use and physical improvements, and have lapsed into inactivity on the grounds that since no funds were available to finance physical improvements, there was nothing for planning boards to do. Probably the majority of planning boards in the Region confine their activity almost entirely to reviewing subdivision plans and occasional revision of zoning ordinances, with perhaps a completed but rapidly aging master plan reposing on the shelves.

There have been some outstanding jobs of local planning. The Montclair, New Jersey, Planning Board studied and analyzed its city's perplexing problems thoroughly and made important contributions to municipal policy, including an orderly public works and capital budget program which has been in operation for several years. The Rutherford, New Jersey, Planning Board, with the aid of a large WPA appropriation, carried out a thorough study of land use, public utilities, tax and fiscal policy, zoning, traffic and parking needs, etc. The planning boards of Brookhaven and Islip towns in Suffolk County have made themselves vital elements in the governments of their areas through active and intelligent work.

Fort Lee, New Jersey, was placed under the financial control of three business men appointed by the Federal court for a fifteen-year term under a rehabilitation act following municipal bankruptcy. This unique Board of Liquidation for the Borough of Fort Lee, realizing that lack of planned municipal management was largely responsible for the borough's huge burden of prematurely improved areas, asked the Regional Plan Association to undertake planning and rezoning of the community. The resulting Master Plan was published by the Association[1] and the revised zoning ordinance was adopted by the borough officials. Within a year the borough reported that its bonds had been restored to par value, and that long-overdue building activity was getting under way.

Westfield, New Jersey, is outstanding as an example of planning with the aid of the municipal executive personnel. Its town engineer has had the key role in the establishment of excellent financial management, a long-term public works program and capital budget, a careful procedure of weighing each project in terms of first cost, operating and financing cost, and relation to other projects and to town development, and a definite program for rehabilitation of blighted areas.

The impact of depression difficulties has brought home to other municipal officials the need for financial planning, and for the planning approach in engineering departments, particularly in the supervision of subdivisions and the selection of public improvements. Many communities adopted a policy of exclusion of low-cost, low-tax-yielding homes, and it should be noted that while this policy is beneficial locally, from the overall point of view it cannot be regarded as an adequate solution to one of the main problems of economic democracy in metropolitan areas.

In summation, a review of accomplishments or lack of them in local planning in the Region points to the vital need of a functioning staff, concerning itself with the total problem of the municipality and the coordination of the work of each executive branch. The early philosophy of planning organization, function and operation methods has come into serious question. That philosophy conceived the planning agency as concerned almost exclusively with land use and major physical improvements, maintaining a somewhat dis-

trustful, watchdog attitude toward elected officials, and imparting wisdom from a special abode detached from the everyday administration of political offices.

Experience indicates that boards operating on this philosophy have gone to sleep. Successful planning has been characterized by closer contact with the governing body and operating officials, with greater emphasis on the coordinating role; by the provision of expert, full-time personnel; and by a broader conception of the planning function corresponding to the broadened functions of government.

NEIGHBORHOOD PLANNING

Radburn, planned and executed on a full-community scale, has not been duplicated. Instead the revival of building activity was executed by many individual subdivider-builders. If their work has been characterized by persistence of the merchandising principle that every man's home must strive to look like his personal castle, nevertheless planning considerations have received far more attention than in the building of the 1920's. The increased control of subdivision platting which has been made available to local planning agencies in New York State by amendments adopted in 1938 to the planning enabling acts has contributed to this. Even more important, however, has been the influence of the technical staff of the Land Planning Division of the Federal Housing Administration, without whose approval no subdivider can secure FHA mortgage insurance for his purchasers. The land planning office has completely planned the layout of many large developments, and has won over the clan of operative builders from hostility or indifference to understanding and active support of intelligent subdividing principles.

Public housing projects financed by the United States Housing Authority have, by reason of their large scale, been able to ignore the impediments of small lot sizes and arbitrarily imposed street patterns to achieve logical grouping and orientation, and have also been able to incorporate some features of neighborhood design. Parkchester, the Metropolitan Life Insurance Company's apartment city in The Bronx, is the outstanding urban housing achievement by private capital in the Region in the period under review. These accomplishments, though subject to criticism on some points of location and design, should serve to increase public consciousness of the advantages of large-scale planning in residential development.

Neither new subdivisions nor public housing, however, are enough in themselves to correct the costly mistakes in city building of the past. Techniques to release private capital for the task of urban redevelop-

[1] Regional Plan Bulletin No. 53, "A Master Plan for Fort Lee—A Sample Procedure for Rehabilitation of a Community," February 3, 1941.

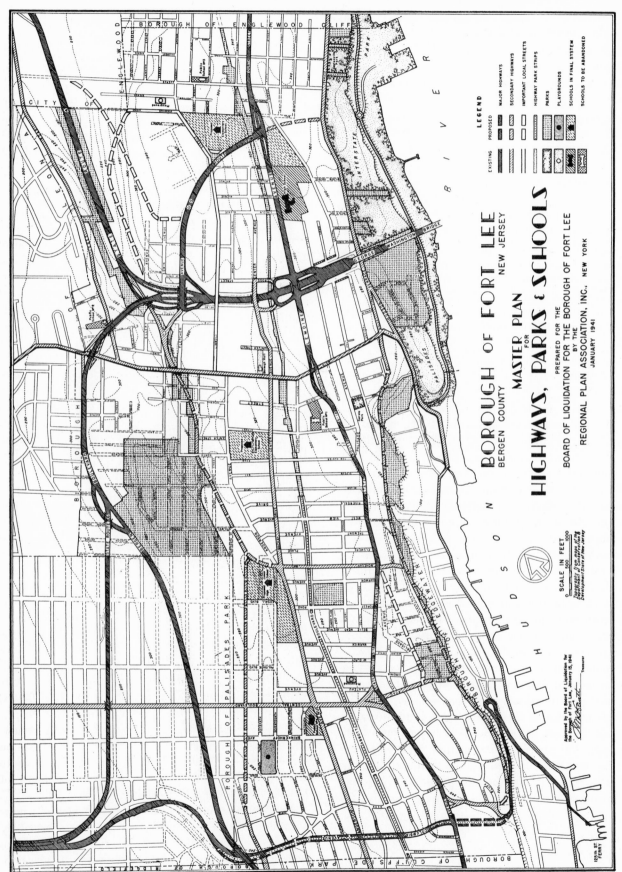

BOROUGH OF FORT LEE
BERGEN COUNTY NEW JERSEY

MASTER PLAN
FOR

HIGHWAYS, PARKS & SCHOOLS

PREPARED FOR THE
BOARD OF LIQUIDATION FOR THE BOROUGH OF FORT LEE
BY THE
REGIONAL PLAN ASSOCIATION, INC., NEW YORK
JANUARY 1941

FIGURE 3

ment are needed. A region-wide Planned Neighborhood Development Conference in March, 1940, was sponsored by the Regional Plan Association and participated in by all the agencies directly concerned.[1] A neighborhood development committee was subsequently appointed by the Board of Directors. It helped initiate, and actively supported passage of, the New York Urban Redevelopment Corporations Law in 1941, which makes it possible for private capital under adequate control to enter the field of reconstruction and rehabilitation with the power of eminent domain plus limited tax exemption, and recognizes the neighborhood unit principle for redevelopment; the law requires that the redevelopment plan must secure the approval of the city planning agency. Support of financial institutions is being mobilized by the Association in readiness for a survey and plan for a post-war neighborhood unit demonstration under this law. Another important step was the passage in 1942 of the Redevelopment Companies Law, which makes practicable the investment of insurance company funds in redevelopment operations under a somewhat different and simplified procedure than that in the Corporations law.

Most recently, initiative has appeared in an important new sector, the head office of the FHA. In December, 1941, this agency published "A Handbook of Urban Redevelopment" in which the neighborhood principle is accorded full recognition and the need for new municipal implements of land control is stressed. FHA personnel have been assigned to a nation-wide follow-up to the handbook, to work out practical local procedures of action in preparation for a post-war rehabilitation effort.

Planning agencies at the neighborhood level, potentially capable of lending energy and guidance to direct action when urban redevelopment planning reaches down to the grass roots, have meanwhile been developing in embryo within neighborhood associations, which are particularly plentiful in New York City. These agencies vary widely in their aims and methods, some existing for promotion or protection of real estate interests, others for improvement of education, social work in health or delinquency, etc., but the activities of an increasing number of them have begun to incorporate the planning approach. More and more of them are attempting overall studies of their area, and there is strong likelihood that several of them may become key agencies for initiation and promotion of redevelopment plans for their neighborhoods.

---

[1] See Regional Plan Bulletin No. 51, "Approval of Neighborhood Unit Development Plan Advances Regional Program of Rehabilitation," July 1, 1940, for a summary of the addresses and reports prepared for the conference.

FEDERAL PLANNING

Other federal agencies besides those already mentioned have made important contributions which have helped to vitalize and promote the cause of planning in the Region. Among the new or expanded agencies of the Federal government which have become a prominent part of American life in the last decade, the great majority aim by positive action rather than negative regulation to sustain employment, stimulate industry, combat poverty, and improve the use of our national resources. These agencies recognize that in order to act they must plan, and in order to plan they must assemble facts. An enormous amount of work has been done in this first stage. It is of particular significance because the basic data which have been gathered are also valuable to planning agencies at other levels of government. Much additional work has been done in analysis of these data through research and planning studies, which have crystallized in publications and the development of expert personnel in each field; these too can assist planning at the state, county and local levels.

The extent of this development is indicated in a publication of the National Resources Planning Board in 1940, entitled "Federal Aids to Local Planning." It contains a description of each Federal agency from which other planning agencies can secure basic statistics, research studies on techniques and administration, technical assistance, etc. Included are 37 agencies in nine major departments, seven independent agencies, and the National Resources Planning Board itself which is part of the Executive Office of the President. From these agencies almost any locality can find out a great deal about itself, particularly about its physical resources and economic activities.

Local and regional offices of Federal agencies have done effective planning work, both directly and indirectly. Outstanding in this connection are the National Resources Planning Board, the Work Projects Administration, the Federal Housing Administration, and the United States Housing Authority (through local authorities), while the war emergency has brought the development of Regional Coordinator's Offices of Defense, Health and Welfare Services (under the Federal Security Agency) and the National Housing Agency.

The NRPB and the ODH&WS are planning agencies by function. The NRPB's regional offices carry out or stimulate local development studies and plans to implement the broad lines of policy established at the national level of research. The New York State ODH&WS, while an emergency agency, has made what may be a permanent contribution to the technique of harmonized, voluntarily coordinated action among diverse governmental agencies, by its active leadership of the Federal-State Advisory Council. In this Council are grouped all agencies whose operations extend to the local level, with the object of establishing mutually consistent objectives and methods, balancing development programs, exchanging information, eliminating overlapping work and authority within each area of activity, and establishing a central agency of contact with local officials.

The WPA, the FHA, and the USHA do planning work not because planning as such is their function, but because it is necessary as a background for their spending activities. By the logic of pay-the-piper-call-the-tune, agencies which allocate or direct funds tend naturally to take over plan making as well. Accordingly, the WPA has carried on in its own state and local branches a great part of the studies of development needs which have guided its selection of projects. The FHA has relied greatly on its own Market Analysis Division for its appraisal of the merits of different localities as areas for new home construction and mortgage investment, while another branch, the Land Planning Division, has applied advanced subdivision layout principles to hundreds of developments.

There has been criticism of the local operations of Federal agencies. It has its roots in the fact that Federal centralization of spending was accompanied by Federal centralization of planning, with the result that decisions affecting local development were made by agencies not sufficiently responsible to local government, and accomplishments were not coordinated with local planning objectives. The Federal agencies reply that, in general, realistic, consistent and detailed local plans were not available to serve as a guide.

More recently there has been a definite trend among Federal agencies themselves to stress decentralized planning, so that local plans may locate federally-financed development. There is a potentiality for teamwork between local agencies with well-thought-out plans, and Federal agencies with funds, national experience and expert personnel. Local planning groups should recognize their obligation to go more than halfway, if need be, to bring this teamwork about, in view of the benefits which should accrue from its achievement on the one hand, and the dangers inherent in leaving full control in the hands of the central government on the other.

WAR AND POST-WAR PLANNING

As the defense emergency developed and became the war emergency, the Association has concentrated its energies increasingly on problems of war-time adjust-

ment and preparedness against post-war depression. Among official planning agencies in the Region, the same trend has been clear.

In May, 1941, the Association, at the request of officials in the Village of Farmingdale, L. I., advised on rezoning to adjust to a new pressure for housing generated by swiftly increasing employment in nearby aircraft plants.

One of the Association's Bulletins was devoted to a discussion of industrial changes resulting from the war effort, protection, defense aids by planning boards, the handling of emergencies on a regional scale, a description of basic regional data available, and a list of the personnel of the Region's defense councils and committees.[1]

The Association cooperated with the Metropolitan Defense Transport Committee in preparation of a regional secondary network of civil highway routes to provide for orderly traffic movement under emergency conditions.

In the closing months of 1941, the Association conducted a survey of housing needs on Staten Island, at the request of the Office of Defense, Health and Welfare Services, and participated in a similar examination of needs in the Bethpage-Farmingdale area.

Concluding that if transportation adjustment were maximized, very little emergency housing would be required in the Region, the Association turned its attention to transportation problems, which became doubly important with the initiation of tire and gasoline rationing. When an official emergency state agency was appointed to deal with this problem in New Jersey, the State Planning Board was assigned the task of gathering and mapping basic data.

The Association has received requests from many branches of the military defense forces for basic data and maps on a region-wide basis, which have been supplied without charge. The topographic model of the Region made by the Association was loaned to the First Army Headquarters at Governor's Island for the duration of the war.

The industrial information developed by the New York State Division of Commerce became of increasing usefulness to the war effort as the need for utilization of all existing capacity became more urgent. In the spring of 1942 the Division of Commerce worked with the War Production Board in its intensified efforts to promote subcontracting and the formation of "pools" of machine tool facilities by small fabricators seeking war contracts.

In general, wherever thorough data have been assem-

---

[1] Regional Plan Bulletin No. 54, "National Defense in the New York Region in Relation to City and Regional Planning," April 7, 1941.

bled and organized by planning agencies it has proved useful to the agencies responsible for civilian defense and war production, housing and transportation. However, war needs have revealed that many planning agencies do not have basic data on their areas in usable form, and that almost all planning agencies are weak in information about the economic activities and resources of their areas. Experience in the areas where war problems of different kinds are pressing has also revealed the need for more aggressive attitudes and action by planning boards, to facilitate the war program and to protect communities against unfortunate consequences of necessarily swift action of Federal agencies, by positive guidance rather than negative resistance.

The overall picture of planning board activity for post-war preparedness is more satisfactory. The development of a reserve shelf of well-considered public works, with the stimulus of the Local Public Works Programming Office of the National Resources Planning Board, and the theme of urban redevelopment, are the two main elements of post-war planning. By May, 1942, 19 municipalities in New Jersey, and five counties and 21 municipalities in southern New York State, had agreed to develop financial planning in cooperation with the program. In New Jersey the State Planning Board, and in New York State a special com-

mittee appointed by Governor Lehman, have been charged with the preparation of a post-war public works program. Planning boards have an opportunity to help guide the public works expenditures which will result from these plans. It is urgent, however, that they develop closer cooperation with governing units if they are to participate in this work. The New York City Planning Commission in May, 1942, published a report which described and mapped recommended projects of the different city departments and the New York City Housing Authority.

Urban redevelopment is a task which should form part of the post-war public works effort and contribute as well to a long-term revival of private building. Its proper execution calls for searching analysis and balanced planning to which all other public improvements should be carefully related. In this task perhaps more than any other, it is a near-certainty that if planning boards do not take the initiative to formulate intelligent local plans, the job will not be done adequately. Yet the costs of blight are at the root of the financial difficulties of the Region's cities, and tend to accelerate the flight of economic activities from urban centers. The economic survival of the New York Region may thus hinge on the spirit and competence with which planning agencies tackle the job of rebuilding our cities.

PUBLICATIONS OF THE REGIONAL PLAN ASSOCIATION

FROM PLAN TO REALITY—ONE.—Four years of Progress on the Regional Development of New York and Its Environs (1933)

FROM PLAN TO REALITY—TWO.—Eight years of Progress on the Regional Development of New York and Its Environs (1938)

FROM PLAN TO REALITY—THREE.—A Third Report of Progress on the Regional Development of New York and Its Environs (1942)

THE REBUILDING OF BLIGHTED AREAS.—A Study of the Neighborhood Unit in Replanning and Plot Assemblage (1933)

TRAFFIC AND PARKING STUDY—CENTRAL BUSINESS DISTRICTS OF NEW YORK CITY (in preparation, July, 1942)

SIXTY REGIONAL PLAN BULLETINS on planning topics related to the Metropolitan Area (1931-1942)

THE REGIONAL PLAN OF NEW YORK AND ITS ENVIRONS

(Sponsored by the Russell Sage Foundation)

SURVEY VOLUMES:

    I. Major Economic Factors in Metropolitan Growth and Arrangement (1928)

    II. Population, Land Values, and Government* (1929)

    III. Highway Traffic (1927)

    IV. Transit and Transportation (1928)

    V. Public Recreation* (1928)

    VI. Buildings: Their Uses and the Spaces about Them (1931)

    VII. Neighborhood and Community Planning* (1929)

    VIII. Physical Conditions and Public Services (1929)

PLAN VOLUMES:

    I. The Graphic Regional Plan (1929)

    II. The Building of the City (1931)

———————

    * *Out of print.*

All of the above publications may be obtained at the office of the Regional Plan Association, 400 Madison Avenue, New York, N. Y. Full information, including prices, will be sent upon request.

RUSSELL SAGE FOUNDATION PUBLICATIONS RELATED TO PLANNING

OUTLINE OF TOWN AND CITY PLANNING, by Thomas Adams (1935)

ZONING, by E. M. Bassett (1936)

THE MASTER PLAN, by E. M. Bassett (1938)

HOUSING FOR THE MACHINE AGE, by Clarence A. Perry (1939)

YOUR COMMUNITY, by Joanna C. Colcord (1939)